DISCOVER·NATURE

in Water
& Wetlands

DISCOVER · NATURE

in Water & Wetlands

Things to Know and Things to Do

Elizabeth P. Lawlor

with illustrations by Pat Archer

STACKPOLE
BOOKS

Published by
STACKPOLE BOOKS
5067 Ritter Road
Mechanicsburg, PA 17055
www.stackpolebooks.com

Printed in the United States of America

Cover illustrations by Pat Archer
Cover design by Wendy A. Reynolds

10 9 8 7 6 5 4 3 2 1

First edition

Library of Congress Cataloging-in-Publication Data

Lawlor, Elizabeth P.
      Discover nature in water and wetlands : things to know and things to do / Elizabeth P. Lawlor ; with illustrations by Pat Archer.
            p.   cm.
      Includes bibliographical references.
      Summary: Introduces the reader to some common plants and animals that can be found in various water environments and provides various related "hands-on" activities.
      ISBN 0-81117-2731-9 (alk. paper)
      1. Freshwater biology—Juvenile literature. 2. Freshwater biology—Experiments—Juvenile literature. [1. Freshwater biology.] I. Archer, Pat, ill. II. Title.

QH96.16 .L38   1999
578.76—dc21   99-044787

To my teachers and students
with gratitude

Four Ducks on a Pond
Four ducks on a pond,
A grass-bank beyond,
A blue sky of spring,
White clouds on the wing,
What a little thing
To remember for years—
To remember with tears

—William Allingham (1824–89)
  Irish poet and critic

CONTENTS

ACKNOWLEDGMENTS

There are many scientists, field researchers, and authors whose help has made this book possible. They gave their time and expertise to the project by willingly sharing their wisdom and knowledge with me. In the course of our conversations, they clarified many points and reconciled conflicting pieces of information sometimes found in the literature. Some of them provided me with valuable reading material in the form of abstracts, papers, and references to relevant research projects. Some took extra time to tell me about their adventures in the field. Those stories added to my appreciation of the creatures and plant life discussed in the pages of this book.

The scientists who helped me are Dr. Peter Rosenbaum, Biology Department, State University of New York, Oswego; Dr. Ken Soltesz, Cranberry Lake Preserve, North White Plains, New York; Dr. Thomas Pauley, Biology Department, Marshall University, Huntington, West Virginia; Dr. Terry Webster, Biological Sciences Group, University of Connecticut, Stores, Connecticut; and Dr. Richard Smith, Applied Physics Laboratory, Johns Hopkins University, Baltimore, Maryland.

I also want to thank my editor at Stackpole Books, Jane Devlin Barrick, for her continued patience and editorial assistance. The list of credits would not be complete if I did not include, once again, Dr. Francis X. Lawlor, who continues to be a constructive critic and is always ready to make at least one suggestion. Thanks again, Frank.

INTRODUCTION

This book, the seventh in the Discover Nature series, is for people who want to find out about the wild things that thrive in ponds and puddles. Like the other volumes in the series, this book is concerned with knowing and doing. It is for people who want to get close to nature. It is for the young, for students, for teachers, for parents, for retirees, for all those with a new or renewed interest in the world around us. Getting started as a naturalist requires a friendly, patient guide; this book is intended to be just that. It is intended to gently lead you to the point of knowledge and experience where various field guides will be useful to you. When you have "done" this book, I hope that you will feel in touch with the plants and creatures that live in wet places.

Each chapter introduces you to a common, easily found living thing that can be found in ponds or puddles and summarizes the major points of interest in the scientific research available. You will learn about its unique place in the web of life and the most fascinating aspects of its lifestyle. Each chapter also suggests activities—things you can do to discover for yourself what each creature or plant looks like, where it lives, and how it survives.

In the first part of each chapter, you will find the important facts about a particular living thing, including some amazing discoveries that scientists have made. You will learn the common names of plants and animals, as well as their scientific names, which are usually Latin. In the second part of each chapter, called "The World of . . ." you will be guided through a series of observational and explanatory activities. This hands-on involvement with plants and animals is certainly the most important of all learning experiences. This is how you will really discover what life in ponds and puddles is all about, something that no amount of reading can do for you.

HOW TO USE THIS BOOK

Feel free to start reading at any point in this book. If you're really interested in dragonflies, for instance, and have a chance to observe them somewhere, read that chapter. Then read "What You Will Need" below and "The World of . . ." section of the chapter. This section also tells you what specific science skills are used in the activity. Do take the suggestion that you keep a field notebook.

My great hope is that this book will be only a beginning for you. I have suggested other readings, keyed to each chapter, to help you learn more than this book can provide. In a sense, when you begin your explorations, you will go beyond all books. Once you get started, Nature herself will be your guide.

WHAT YOU WILL NEED

To become fully involved in the hands-on activities suggested in this book, you'll need very little equipment. Your basic kit requires only a few essentials, starting with a field notebook. I generally use a spiral-bound, five-by-seven-inch memo book. Throw in several ballpoint pens and some pencils and a flexible ruler. Include a small magnifier or hand lens. Nature centers generally stock good plastic lenses that cost a few dollars. You may want to have a bug box—a small, see-through acrylic box with a magnifier permanently set into the lid. It's handy for examining spiders, beetles, and other small creatures; with it you can capture, hold, and study them without touching or harming them. A penknife and several small sandwich bags are also useful to have on hand.

All the basic kit contents easily fit into a medium-size Ziploc bag, ready to carry in a backpack, bicycle basket, or glove compartment.

Basic Kit:
field notebook
ruler
magnifier or hand lens
bug box
penknife
pens and pencils
small sandwich bags

Although not essential, a pair of binoculars adds to the joy of discovery when you are exploring. You may also want a camera and lenses for taking pictures. A three-ringed loose-leaf notebook is helpful for recording, in expanded form, the information you collect in the field. As you make notes, you'll have an opportunity to reflect on what you saw and think through some of the questions raised during your explorations. Consult your reference books and field guides for additional information.

As you read and investigate, you will come to understand how fragile these communities of living things can be, and you will inevitably encounter the effects of humankind's presence. I hope you will become concerned in specific, practical ways and will seek to help make a difference for the future of the environment. We still have a long way to go.

PART I
THE STAGE

CHAPTER 1

Water

A LIFE-GIVING LIQUID

It is a bitterly cold winter morning. An icy wind whips across the snow-covered field, leaving a cloud of powdery snow in its wake. The sun's rays make miniature sparkling rainbows on the ice-encased tree branches. A few hours have passed since the hockey players left the warmth of their homes. They are thirsty and chilled. It's time to seek shelter in the shed, where each left a snack and a thermos filled with a warm drink before the game began. When the thermos bottles of hot liquid are opened, clouds of steam rush into the cold air.

During this short span of time, the players have experienced the varied phases of water: solid, liquid, and gas. Each of these watery expressions is essential for life as we know it. Water makes up about 70 percent of our body mass, and it transports essential vitamins and minerals throughout our bodies. Plants and other animals have similar needs for water. Water covers about three-fourths of the earth's surface, and about 97 percent of it is found in the oceans. About 2 percent is locked in ice as glaciers and ice caps. Only about 0.7 percent is in freshwater lakes, ponds, rivers, and underground streams.

The chemical formula for water is H_2O, meaning that a molecule of water is made up of two atoms of hydrogen and one atom of oxygen. The oxygen atom and the two hydrogen atoms bond very strongly to form one water molecule, a bond which is difficult to break. What you may have forgotten is that there are additional, weaker attractions between oxygen and hydrogen that cause adjacent water molecules to form weak but important bonds with each other. Water molecules connect weakly to other water molecules by the attraction of the hydrogen atoms in one molecule to oxygen atoms in other molecules. This bonding results in loosely arranged and unstable chains that give water its fluid nature.

This structure of water molecules gives water an array of remarkable qualities. Water freezes at 32 degrees Fahrenheit (0 degrees Celsius) and boils at 212 degrees F. (100 degrees C.). If water lacked those weak hydrogen bonds holding the molecules together, it would boil at minus 112 degrees F. (80 degrees C.) and freeze at minus 148 degrees F. (minus 100 degrees C.). Life under these conditions would be impossible, because there would be no liquid water at normal earth temperatures—no oceans, no lakes, no rivers, and no essential body fluids.

Water has many other characteristics essential for life. It responds more slowly to changes in air temperature than other liquids. If you live in the Northeast and have gone swimming late in the spring in the ocean or a lake, you have experienced this phenomenon. Although the temperature of the air is

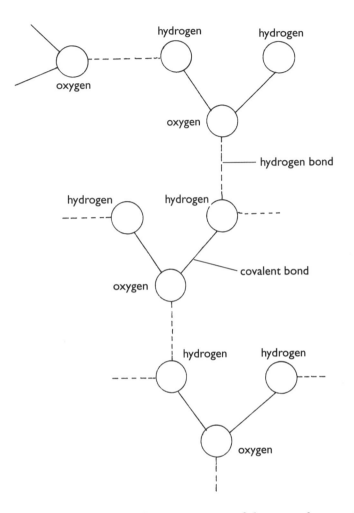

generally rising at this season, the temperature of the water has not increased accordingly. Your dive into the water leaves no doubt about this. The reverse is true in the fall. Bodies of water will still be warm enough for swimming through September and perhaps into October, although there may be a definite chill in the air. This is why bays, lakes, and other bodies of water are called "heat sinks." Water stores heat, acting like a giant reservoir that evens out temperature fluctuations on our planet. This occurs because the hydrogen bonds that link water molecules together help water absorb a large amount of heat before there is a change in its temperature. Once the temperature of water has risen, it is slow to release this heat as the air temperature cools.

Like most other substances, water shrinks when it cools. However, when it drops to 39 degrees F. (3.89 degrees C.), water ceases to shrink and begins to expand. Continued cooling results in continued expansion. Water below this temperature is less dense, and therefore lighter, than an equal amount of warmer water; this makes ice float.

As winter approaches, surface water cools down, becoming dense and heavy. It sinks to the bottom of the pond, pushing up the warmer water beneath it. This water cools at the surface, becoming dense and heavy, and it sinks. At some point, the whole pond will be about 39 degrees. Now, as the surface water continues to cool, it no longer sinks but stays at the surface, where it continues to cool until it reaches 32 degrees F. (0 degrees C.), the freezing point of water. From the moment the water temperature dropped to 39 degrees F. (3.89 degrees C.), it began to expand. As it continued to cool it became lighter. The result of this is that water colder than 39 degrees F. and ice both float.

If the weather is really cold, the surface ice will get thicker and thicker. This is good insulation that prevents the deeper water from freezing. Only a shallow pond will freeze to the bottom.

In the spring, the sun and the warming air combine to melt the surface layer of ice. The lighter ice keeps floating up over the warmer meltwater, exposing the cold ice to the warmer air, which then melts and is pushed aside by the lighter ice, until the whole body of water is again liquid at 39 degrees F. After this, the surface water continues to warm up, while the deeper areas remain quite cold, but not colder than 39 degrees.

If this process did not take place, the bottoms of ponds would remain frozen all year, and each winter would add to the bottom ice, until only a thin surface layer of water would melt each summer.

These properties of water protect aquatic plants and animals from rapid and potentially destructive temperature changes. Fish can continue to live in the cold yet unfrozen pond water that lies beneath the layer of ice.

The change in the density of water as it warms and cools has important side effects for the life in ponds. In late fall, as winter approaches and water becomes denser and sinks to the bottoms of ponds, it carries with it dissolved oxygen and nutrients. This action replenishes supplies of vital nutrients used up during the summer. In the spring, the process is reversed, as warmer air begins to melt the pond ice. When the meltwater reaches 39 degrees, it is most dense and it sinks. Once again, the pond water circulates, carrying more oxygen to the depths and distributing nutrients. This fall and spring circulation is crucial to life throughout the pond. Without this seasonal circulation, the depths would be starved of oxygen, and nutrients would settle in the sediment and not be available to life in all layers of the water. Eventually it would die, and the pond would be lifeless.

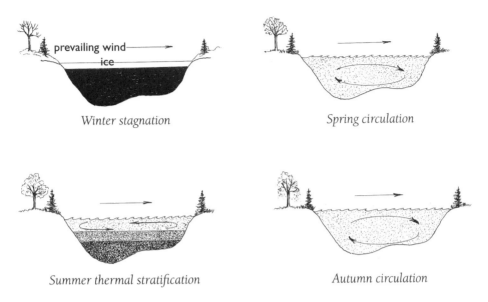

Winter stagnation

Spring circulation

Summer thermal stratification

Autumn circulation

During spring and autumn, the circulation in a pond or lake carries dissolved oxygen to deeper water and nutrients to shallower water.

Another fascinating characteristic of water is its ability to form a "skin." You can see this working in a drop of water. The surface of the drop is curved because the water molecules are attached to each other but not to the surrounding air or to the surface on which the drop is sitting. The attraction of water molecules to each other is also responsible for the "rubbery" surface on a pond or puddle, a naturally occurring "trampoline" strong enough to support insect life such as whirligig beetles and water striders. Mosquito larvae and other waterbound life forms use the underside of the surface "skin."

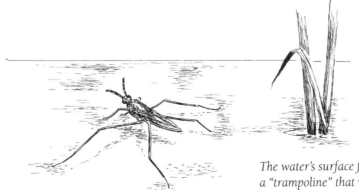

The water's surface forms a "trampoline" that water striders can walk on.

Water has many additional properties or characteristics that make it unique and that are essential to the life of plants and animals. You can discover some of them by doing the activities suggested below.

THE WORLD OF WATER

What you will need

basic kit
2 glasses of similar size and shape
various liquids: water, alcohol,
    vegetable oil, honey
salt
4 medicine droppers
food coloring
tea bags
medium-size jar

waxed paper
paper towels
cardboard
paper clip
needle
detergent
celery stick with leaves
plastic strawberry container
leaf

Science skills

observing
recording

inferring

OBSERVATIONS

Water has no smell or taste. It is colorless and transparent. It is commonplace. It is remarkable. Many scientists who have made water the focus of their life's work began with simple observations and questions that led to more complex investigations. You can do some interesting things with water and explore its properties in the following activities. The explanations for each property are based on the behavior of molecules. Write down your understanding of the explanation for what happens in each investigation. Include diagrams when you think they will be helpful. Try to come up with additional investigations that will probe these properties. Can you apply your discoveries to plant and animal life in the water?

Water: A Dissolving Agent. Many kinds of minerals and nutrients are washed into the pond by way of rain runoff. These materials do not settle on the bottom of the pond because water is an excellent solvent, capable of dissolving mineral matter, much of which is then absorbed by plant life, which in turn is eaten by animals living in the water.

1. When a substance dissolves in water, the substance disappears and the water remains clear, although in some cases it is clear but takes on a color.

Put about three cups of warm water (twenty-four ounces) into a glass jar. Add a tea bag. As the molecules of tea fill the spaces between the water molecules, the water becomes tea colored. This mixture of tea and water is called a solution.

If you add some sugar to the solution, the sugar molecules will fill the spaces between the water and tea molecules. The new solution is a sweet tea. Is the solution clear?

2. Some substances do not dissolve in water, but remain as small particles suspended in the water. In a suspension, the water is not clear. Muddy water in a pond or lake is a suspension in which the particles of soil do not dissolve in the water. When you look at a pond, puddle, lake, or stream, you can see right away if there is anything in suspension. If the water is clear, there are usually minerals in solution, but this is not so easy to determine. Milk is another example of a suspension.

Sun tea results when water draws out tea molecules and disperses them in water warmed by the sun.

Density. Density is a science concept that relates closely to our everyday experiences. If you have two same-size solid blocks of wood (or metal or any other material) and one is heavier than the other, the heavier one is more dense. If the block is heavier than an identical block of water, it will sink in water. Certain kinds of wood, such as ebony, will sink, and some rocks, like volcanic pumice, will float.

Minerals dissolved in water increase its density. Salt water, for example, is more dense than an equal volume of fresh water. Temperature also has an effect on the density (weight) of water. The warmer water becomes, the less dense, or lighter in weight, it is.

1. To investigate the effect of mineral matter on the density of water, mix a few tablespoons of salt in a glass half filled with water. Stir to help dissolve the salt. Half fill another glass of similar size and shape with water, and add a few drops of food coloring. Tip the glass holding the salt water, and with a medicine dropper, gently add some of the colored water to the salt solution. What happens?

2. The temperature of water also affects its density. Half fill one glass with hot water and another with cold water. Add a few drops of food coloring to the cold water. Using a medicine dropper, carefully add some of the colored cold water to the hot water. What happens? How does the temperature of the water affect its density?

Cohesion. The force that causes molecules to stick together is called cohesion.

1. Compare the cohesive force of some common liquids, such as rubbing alcohol, soapy water, vegetable oil, and tap water.

You will need four medicine droppers and a piece of waxed paper about four by six inches. With a medicine dropper, place a drop or two of each liquid on the waxed paper. Be sure to use the same number of drops for each liquid. Which liquid forms the highest heap? The lowest? Each drip is three dimensional. It is round and when looked at from the side it can vary from a half sphere to a flat pancake shape. If a liquid has strong cohesive forces the drop will be high—almost a half sphere. As the cohesive force diminishes, the drop flattens. How do the drops of these liquids compare? How does the cohesive force of water compare to the cohesive forces of the other liquids? Try this investigation with a thick liquid such as molasses or honey. How does it compare to the liquids you have tested?

2. Fill a glass with water, but do not wet the rim of the glass. With a medicine dropper, very carefully add more water to the glass, drop by drop. Count the drops. How many did you add to the glass that was already full?

Eventually a bulge of water will extend above the glass. A "skin" forms on the top of the water due to the cohesive property of water molecules. It prevents the water from spilling over the rim of the glass.

3. To observe what happens when the cohesive force between water molecules is broken down, you'll need one of those green plastic containers that strawberries are sold in. Fill a dishpan with about three inches of water. Place the strawberry container gently on the surface of the water. What happens? To the water, add a few drops of detergent. What happens? What does the detergent do to the surface tension of water? Detergents break down the cohesive force between water molecules. Since these forces were what kept the basket on the surface, the basket does a nosedive. Breaking the cohesive bonds that hold molecules of water to each other is useful in the washing machine or dishwasher. There are more water molecules available to make an object wetter. However, this effect is not so useful in a pond or stream: Detergent in pond water will adversely affect the insects that travel on its surface. Floating plants such as duckweed will experience similar problems. The detergent disrupts the life cycles of these and other life forms.

Rubbery Skin. One hot summer day, I was lying on an old dock on a small pond. As I looked down on the calm mirror of muddy water, an insect with long legs moved along on the surface of the water. Each of the creature's feet seemed to make a dimple in the surface of the water, and the bug did not sink or get wet. How interesting! I later found out that something called surface tension allows insects to skate across a pond or puddle, and this is caused by the cohesion of water molecules. Some insects swim underwater like fish; others travel on the surface. Do you think that surface-traveling insects have an advantage over their swimming counterparts? Are there disadvantages?

You can investigate the strength of this skin with a container of water, a paper clip, and a needle. Bend the paper clip to make an L shape. Support the needle on the foot of the L, and gently rest it on the surface of the water. Carefully remove the paper clip. What happens? You can also try this using your fingers. Can you float the paper clip? Imagine that this is a pond or a puddle and the needle is a water boatman or some other surface-dwelling insect. Now pollute the "pond" with a sprinkle of detergent. Describe and then explain what happened. What are the ramifications of this for a larger living system?

Adhesion. Water molecules not only stick to each other, but also will stick to molecules in other objects. This characteristic is called adhesion. You have felt the effects of adhesion when removing a Band-Aid from a wound.

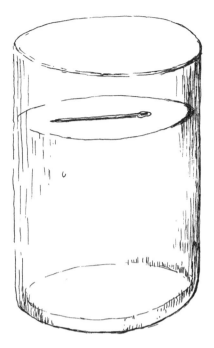

A needle can float on the water's surface due to the tendency of water molecules to stick together.

Liquids such as honey, vegetable oil, tap water, and soapy water also display adhesive qualities. To compare the adhesive qualities of different liquids, you will need to make an incline of waxed paper. Put the edge of the paper on a piece of stiff cardboard, with one edge raised by a couple of books so that the paper slopes downward. Place a drop of each liquid in a row at the top of the waxed paper slope. Describe what happens. Are some of the liquids faster than others? Make a drawing of the path each liquid takes as it moves down the incline. Which liquid has the greatest sticking action? The least? Try this with other liquids.

Capillary Action. Under certain conditions, the combined forces of adhesion and cohesion work together to create capillary action. Clinical laboratory technicians rely on capillary action when they take blood samples. When doing the work, the technician touches the tip of a narrow glass tube (a capillary tube) to a drop of blood from the patient's fingertip. The drop zips up the tube—capillary action at work.

Capillary action is one factor that causes water to rise in plants from the roots up through extremely narrow tubes. It is also why cotton and other materials soak up liquids.

In the wetlands and woodlands you visit, the properties of adhesion and cohesion of water are constantly at work all around you. Underfoot, the processes move water through the soil, into the layers of decaying leaves, into the cracks in the rocks. At every point, life is affected: animal life, insect life, plant life, microbial life.

1. Advertisers try to persuade us to buy one paper towel over another because one absorbs liquid faster. You can use the properties of capillary action to investigate these claims for yourself. Cut strips of equal length and width (about two inches wide and twelve inches long) from several different brands of paper towels. Tape the strips to the edge of a table or to a cabinet above the kitchen counter. Fill a rectangular container with water, and position it under the strips so that an inch or two of the paper is in the water. Be

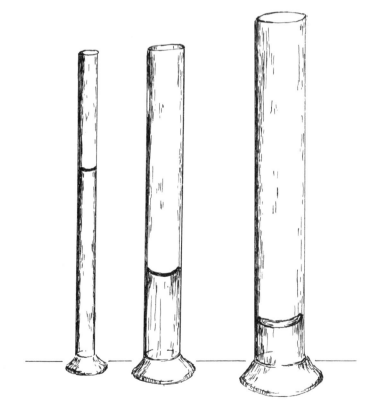

Capillary action at work. The more narrow the tube, the higher the water will rise, up to a point.

sure the strips are at the same depth. How high does the water go in each of the strips? How long did it take for the water to reach that height? What do you conclude from this investigation?

2. To observe how a plant uses capillary action, you will need a celery stalk with leaves. Remove a stalk of celery from the bulb. With a knife, remove about two inches of the stalk above the flared end. Put a few inches of water in a glass. Add enough food coloring to make a deeply colored solution. Immerse the celery stalk into the colored solution. In a day, you will see the colored water rising in the stalk. Capillary action is one reason why this happens.

Evaporation and Condensation. Spilled water disappears, wet clothes dry on a line, and sidewalk puddles vanish. The process responsible is called evaporation. Evaporation is the changing of liquid water to invisible water vapor, and it occurs through the action of heat.

You can observe this happening by half filling two glasses with water. Mark the level of the water in each glass with a fine-line marker. Place one glass on a windowsill, where the combined heat from the sun and the house heating system will cause evaporation to take place. Place the second glass in a cool place away from sunlight. Leave both glasses in place for several days. Make a mark on each glass that shows the water level each day. At the end of several days, what is the difference in the water level in the two glasses? Did the rate of evaporation vary according to where you put the glasses?

COMPARING RATES OF WATER EVAPORATION

Number of Days	Amount of Water Lost (inches)	
	Glass 1 (on windowsill)	Glass 2 (cool, dark place)
1		
2		
3		
4		
5		

One factor that affects the rate of evaporation is the amount of heat applied to the water. You can speed up the process considerably by heating water in a kettle on the stove. The heat turns the water into vapor. The steam itself is invisible; this water vapor becomes visible only when condensed as water droplets in the air. As the steam contacts the cooler air, tiny droplets of water vapor form. We see these droplets as a cloud forming a little beyond the spout of the kettle.

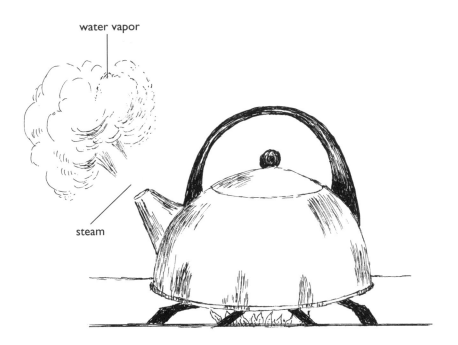

water vapor

steam

When heat is removed, steam will return to liquid water, in the process known as condensation. This can happen slowly or very quickly. If you place a relatively cool spoon in or at the edge of the steam cloud, water droplets will appear on the spoon. When you try this, do not get your fingers too close to the cloud, or you may get burned.

The Water Cycle. The process of liquid water changing to a gas and back to a liquid is called the water cycle. You may have seen the water cycle at work if you own an aquarium. As the water in the aquarium warms, the liquid is changed to invisible water vapor. When the water vapor comes in contact with the cool glass plate on top of the tank, it changes back to liquid water. You can see this water as droplets on the underside of the glass. The rate of evaporation and condensation is proportional to the amount of heat added to or removed from the system.

The evaporation-condensation cycle is a vital process. On a large scale, it is a primary factor in weather, causing rain, snow, clouds, hurricanes, and tornadoes. It moves water from the oceans to ponds, streams, and lakes. Water evaporates from these bodies into the air and forms clouds. Condensation occurs, producing rain. This water eventually returns to the oceans. It leads to erosion of land, weathering of rocks, and the movement of mountains to the sea.

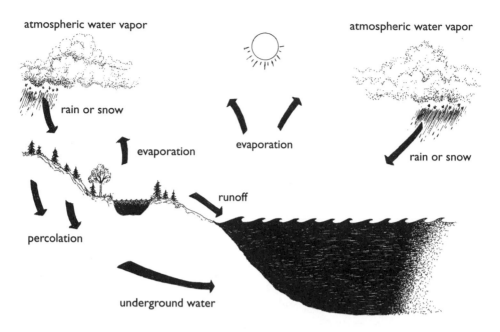

The water cycle: When water evaporates from streams, rivers, and oceans, it forms clouds. The water condenses and returns to the earth as rain and other forms of precipitation.

On a smaller scale, each plant moves water from the soil to nourish leaves and then to the air, where it evaporates. On a hot day, a large tree can move a ton of water from the soil to the air. The dew you see on the grass in the morning is condensed water vapor that was in the air during the day. As the night air cooled the water vapor, it condensed to liquid water. Tons of water return to the grasses overnight as condensed dew, which nourishes the insects and moderates temperature differences in the woodlands.

In the summer, find a leaf from a tree or shrub. Place the leaf in a plastic sandwich bag and seal it. Leave the bag in a sunny place for a day or two, and water droplets will appear inside.

PART II

THE PLAYERS

CHAPTER 2

Trees

WETLAND OAKS

In the early-morning hours, we slipped our canoe into the dark water of the slow-moving stream. The air was chilly and carried with it a warning of frosty mornings to come. Silence pervaded the wetland, and the trees arching over the water gave a sense of remoteness and isolation. Following the stream's meandering course, we passed different hardwood trees whose leaves began to tell of the season's change. Many showed signs of fading greens that would soon yield to the spectacular autumn colors.

Many of the trees we passed were those special oaks that are characteristic of the wetlands, and they made us think of the symbolic ways oak trees have been part of human history. In many cultures, they have stood for strength and determination. They have inspired myths, legends, and imagination. Oak trees have been part of our material world as well. We enjoy their beautiful grain patterns in our furniture, and many of us rely on the strength of oak wood in tool handles, boats, buckets, barrels, and the posts and beams and doors of our homes. The word *oak* has become equated with reliable strength and steadfastness.

The oaks belong to the genus *Quercus,* derived from the Celtic *quer* meaning "beautiful" and *cues,* "tree." During the summer, we picnic in the broad shadows of these green trees, which in the fall become rich reds, oranges, and browns.

Over the past twenty years, scientists have been constructing models to study drought cycles and the effects of acid rain on tree growth. Through a process called cross dating, researchers can construct climatic maps to determine whether a climatic condition is normal for an area or is an aberration. They're also discovering that the presence of trace metals, such as iron, aluminum, titanium, and copper, in the wood of trees may help determine past and present surges in air pollution. Through the patient efforts of researchers in dendrology, the study of trees, we now know about events that occurred as long ago as 6000 B.C.

A well-known characteristic shared by all trees is the pattern of concentric circles seen when a tree is cut down. These ring patterns are most obvious and easily studied on the wood of deciduous trees—trees that shed their leaves each fall. Leonardo da Vinci (1452–1519) first made the connection between the number of rings and the age of a tree, but the mechanism that produces the rings was not clearly understood until more recently. In 1901 Andrew Douglas began the first systematic analysis of tree rings. His extensive work in the area contributed a great deal to what is known today about tree growth.

A tree grows at the tips of the roots and in the buds at the tips of twigs and branches. In those places, delicate developing tissue called meristem is found. When triggered by hormones, the meristem develops and causes the twigs and roots to grow longer.

A tree also grows in circumference. Responsible for this growth is the vascular cambium, a thin layer of tissue only two or three cells thick that lies beneath the bark and covers the entire tree from the smallest rootlets to the most delicate branches. Through the action of cell division in the vascular cambium, all parts of the tree become thicker.

Toward the end of winter, longer and longer periods of daylight trigger the manufacture of growth hormones, such as auxin and gibberellin, by embryonic tissue located in the leaf buds at the ends of twigs and branches. The growth hormones cause developing cells to grow and divide, adding length to the branches and height to the tree. At the root ends, similar events result in longer roots.

At about the same time, the growth hormones produced in the twigs and branches activate the girth-producing vascular cambium. The cells of the vascular cambium produce a system of tubes that develop toward the inside of the tree. These tubes, called xylem, form microscopic pipelines that carry water and nutrients from the soil to the food-producing green leaves. In the spring, when hormonal activity is high, the newly formed xylem cells are large and have thin walls. They make up the springwood, or sapwood, the light component of an annual ring.

Later in the summer, growth hormones are no longer produced by the developing (meristematic) tissues. The vascular cambium reacts to this lack of chemical activity by producing smaller cells with thick walls. These form darker bands of summerwood, or latewood. This cycle of xylem cell production is repeated every year. Together, the light bands of sapwood and the darker bands of latewood form the annual growth rings.

In the fall, when growth slows, the older xylem cells die and fill with lignin and other substances that produce rigidity in the tree. They become part of the nonliving heartwood of the tree. Dead wood makes up almost 99 percent of the tree's volume. In an oak tree, the sapwood and latewood constitute a dense, heavy, strong wood that is much heavier than softwoods such as pine. Some oak trees produce such strong wood that the trees were once reserved for shipbuilding. A kind of oak called the live oak was once used for the outer layer of warships' hulls to serve as armor against enemy cannonballs.

The vascular cambium also produces another system of tubes that develops toward the outside of the tree. After several weeks, these cells mature and

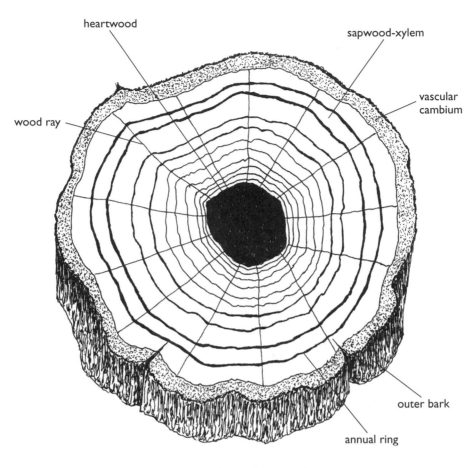

heartwood

sapwood-xylem

vascular cambium

wood ray

outer bark

annual ring

Segment of an oak tree trunk

cease dividing. Stiffened with cellulose, older cells become specialized into hollow, food-carrying tubes called phloem. The phloem system transports carbohydrates manufactured in the green leaves to the branches, trunk, and roots. As the phloem cells age, new cells replace them and push them toward the outside of the tree. The old cells eventually become part of the outer bark.

Lying beneath the outer bark is a thin inner bark, known as the cork cambium. This inner bark produces clusters of cork cells. As the girth of the tree increases, old cork is sloughed off and becomes a secondary component of the bark in many trees. Trees with rough-textured bark produce many short-lived cork cells. Each new batch of cork cells pushes the old cork to the outside, causing them to stretch, crack, and tear. The result of changes in the cork cambium and the expansion of the tree's girth are the rough ridges and ragged furrows that are distinguishing characteristics in the bark of particular trees. The bark of the oak tree is not particularly distinctive to the amateur naturalist, however.

You can get an idea of the relationship between the inner and outer bark if you tear a small strip of bark from a fallen log. The piece you have removed contains both the inner and outer bark of the tree. If a ring of bark is torn all the way around the circumference of a tree, an essential part of the tree's food-transport system is removed, and the tree above the denuded section will eventually starve. Without such interference, as old phloem cells die, replacements are supplied by the vascular cambium. There is no lasting damage, because the rate of new cell formation compensates for the number of cells that have died.

Healthy, intact bark guards trees from invasion by boring insects, fungi, bacteria, molds, and other invaders that can damage the tree or shorten its life. In the cold months, bark protects trees from drying out and from abrupt changes in temperatures. The bark also helps keep hungry mice and deer from nibbling on softer young trees and shrubs.

Occasionally, you may run across a splintered tree bearing a blackened scar of a lightning strike, vivid evidence that even the mighty oaks are no match for an enemy that strikes at random from the sky. The mineral-laden moisture carried in the living cells of the tree from the roots to the highest branches readily conducts electrical energy and provides a pathway from the raised branches to the buried roots. When a huge electrical surge follows this pathway, it generates very high temperatures that can explode the wood fibers and destroy the tree. In a split second, lightning can reduce a tree to a pile of splinters.

Yet some trees, most notably beech, are resistant to lightning strikes because of the oily nature of the wood, which makes them poor conductors of electricity. About one hundred years ago, a study of trees in a German forest investigated the susceptibility of different types of trees to lightning strikes. In the fifty thousand acres of forest studied, oak trees, because of their high water content, fared worse than pine, fir, or beech trees. Oak trees are about sixty times more likely to be struck by lightning than the oily beech.

Oak trees produce a large taproot and some ancillary vertical roots, but the majority of the tree's root system extends horizontally below the surface and can extend some fifty feet beyond the base of the tree. In an electrical storm, this wide root system can pose as much danger as the tree itself to a person walking over these potential "live wires." During an electrical storm, never seek shelter under any tree, but be especially wary of those beautiful oaks.

THE WORLD OF WETLAND TREES

What you will need   **Science skills**

    basic kit   *observing*

    crayons   *inferring*

    camera   *comparing*

OBSERVATIONS

In order to survive in wet places, the trees that live there must be well adapted to special conditions. Saturated soils, especially those that are flooded most of the year, are low in oxygen content and are also highly acidic. These variables make the wetlands a hostile environment for plant growth and reproduction. However, some species of trees survive under these conditions and encounter less competition there than in drier places. Wetland trees are able to tolerate what other tree species cannot. Various types of oak trees are splendidly adapted for survival in the wetlands. The following activities will introduce you to these special oaks.

Although oak trees are featured in this activity, they are not the only trees that flourish in wet places. Eastern cottonwood, red maple, black willow, sweet gum, eastern sycamore, and black ash also thrive in wet or moist areas, and you will have an opportunity to get to know them as well.

Oak Groups. Oak trees are divided into two groups: white oaks and red oaks (sometimes called black oaks). Oak trees interbreed and produce many hybrids. Despite this interbreeding, you can use certain characteristics of their leaves to distinguish one group from another. White oak leaves have rounded lobes, are rough in texture, and have a lighter undersurface. Red oak leaves have angular lobes that end in sharp points, and the upper and lower surfaces feel almost equally smooth. You will discover these characteristics as you explore the world of wetland oaks.

1. White oak leaves
   a. rounded lobes
      overcup oak (*Q. lyrata*)
   b. smooth edge
      water oak (*Q. nigra*)

willow oak (*Q. phellos*)
laurel oak (*Q. laurifolia*)
swamp white oak (*Q. bicolor*)
swamp chestnut oak (*Q. michauxii*)
c.   feel rough
2.   Red oak leaves
a.   pointed lobes with bristle tips
pin oak (*Q. palustris*)
b.   feel smooth

Oak Flowers. The male pollen-bearing flowers dangle from the twig like beads on a string but are not very conspicuous. Several strings hang down from the same point on the twig, making an attractive cascade of tiny flowers. Look for these flowers on the trees in May or June.

The female flowers, called pistillate, are inconspicuous at the angle between the upper surface of the leaves and the stem. This angle is called the axil. They are on the same branches as the pollen-bearing flowers. Pollination occurs when the breeze-dispersed pollen from the male flower falls on the stigma of the female flower.

Late winter through early spring is a good time to begin examining tree

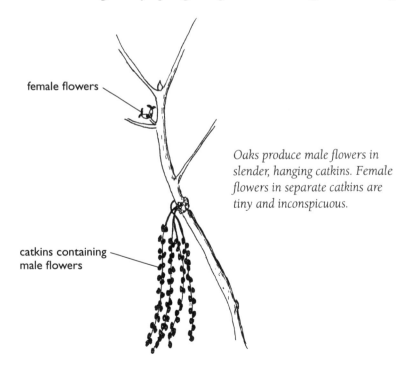

female flowers

catkins containing
male flowers

Oaks produce male flowers in slender, hanging catkins. Female flowers in separate catkins are tiny and inconspicuous.

buds. See the planting zone map to determine the best time to begin examining buds on oaks and the other trees that grow in wet places in your area. If you live in Boston, for example, you are in zone 3, and the buds will begin to swell in late February. Shortly thereafter, you can begin exploring their development. You can get specific information about your zone from county, state, or federal agricultural agencies or extension services of state universities.

FLOWER BLOSSOM CHART

Name	Time of Bloom	Flowers Appear
1. swamp white oak		when leaves are half grown
2. laurel oak		
3. pin oak		when leaves are half grown
4. willow oak		when leaves are small
5. eastern cottonwood		before leaves
6. red maple		before leaves
7. sweet gum		when leaves are half grown
8.		
9.		
10.		

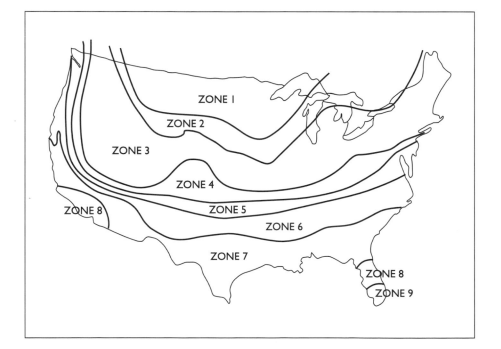

Oak Leaves. The leaves of oak trees often show a great variety in design, not only on different trees, but also on the same tree. To add to the confusion, oak trees tend to hybridize, which sometimes makes distinguishing their leaves a puzzle even to professionals. You may find this annoying when you begin your study of oak leaves, but a little effort will generate a large return in satisfaction.

Look for the following characteristics: Do the leaves feel rough or smooth? Do they resemble feathers? Are the lobes rounded or pointed? Are there spines or bristles at the tips of the lobes? Are the edges of the leaf wavy, do they have teeth, or are they smooth?

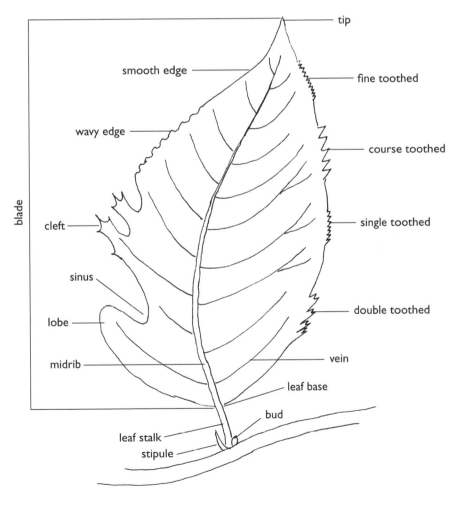

Leaf terminology

The accompanying illustrations show the most common leaf shape for each kind of oak.

Swamp White Oak (*Q. bicolor*). The leaves of this tree are dark green above, silvery below, and irregularly lobed. Feel rough.

Swamp Chestnut Oak (*Q. michauxii*). This tree has simple, broad, three- to five-inch leaves that are dark green and shiny above, light green and hairy below. Margins have regular rounded teeth, which are smaller as they reach the tip. Feel rough.

Swamp white oak
(Quercus bicolor)

Swamp chestnut oak
(also known as Basket oak)
(Quercus michauxii)

Overcup Oak (*Q. lyrata*). This tree has oblong, dark green leaves that are narrow at the base, divided into five to nine lobes, and have irregular sinuses. Feel rough.

Water Oak (*Q. nigra*). Leaves are dull bluish green above and paler below. Smooth and shiny on both surfaces, except for tufts of hair in the axils of veins beneath. Feel rough.

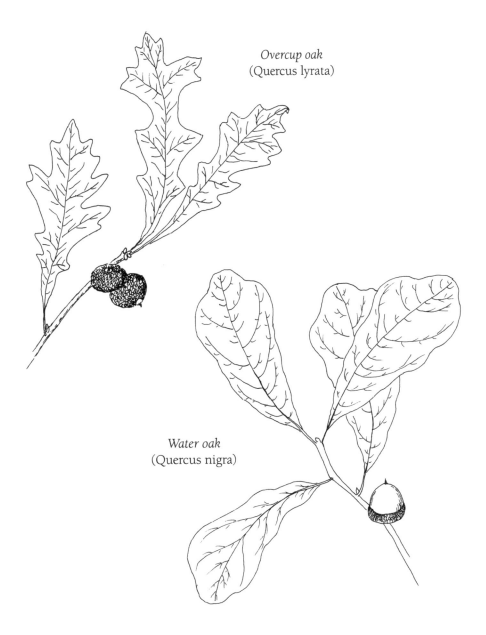

Overcup oak
(Quercus lyrata)

Water oak
(Quercus nigra)

Willow Oak (*Q. phellos*). Leaves are narrow and willowlike, tapered at both ends. Light green and shiny above, dull and paler green below. Obvious network of veins. Feel rough.

Pin Oak (*Q. palustris*). Leaves have five to seven deep, pointed lobes rounded at the base. Dark green, smooth, and shiny above, pale beneath with tufts of hair where major veins meet. Papery texture. Feel smooth.

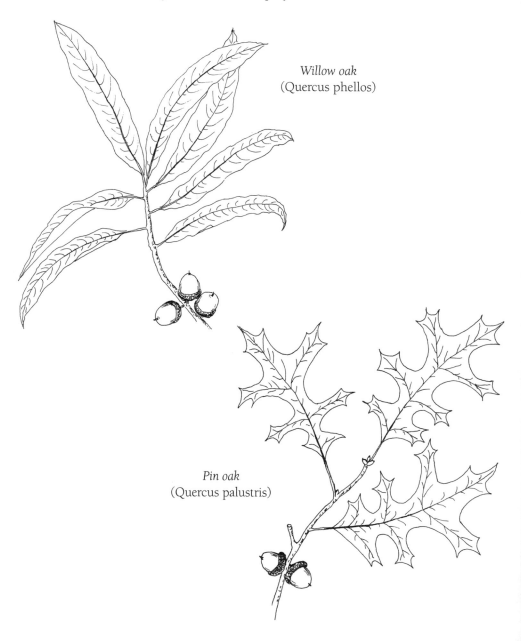

Willow oak
(Quercus phellos)

Pin oak
(Quercus palustris)

Laurel oak
(Quercus laurifolia)

Laurel Oak (*Q. laurifolia*). This tree has deep green leaves three to four inches long that remain on the tree into the winter. Narrow, about one-half inch wide in the middle, tapering at both ends. Feel rough.

Acorns. Acorns, with their scaly caps, are easy to find in the autumn. Collect some acorns that have fallen from a variety of oak trees, and put them into plastic sandwich bags, one acorn from one type of tree per bag. With the help of the illustrations below, determine what types of oak tree each acorn came from. How are acorns from different types of oak trees similar? How do they differ? Do you feel confident identifying the type of oak tree from the acorn? What other characteristics should you look at when trying to identify a tree?

Acorns come in a variety of colors, from the yellow of the chestnut oak, to the russet of the black oak, to the rich wine or deep brilliant red of other oaks. How many different colors did you find?

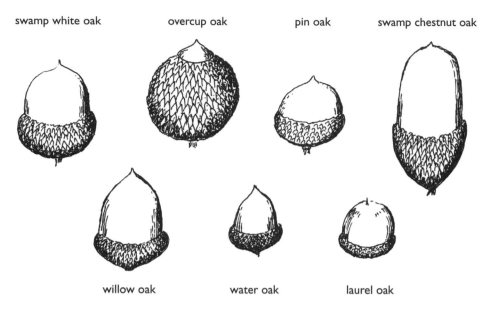

swamp white oak   overcup oak   pin oak   swamp chestnut oak

willow oak   water oak   laurel oak

All oaks have acorns for fruit. Every tree that produces acorns is an oak of one group or another.

Open an acorn to expose the nut within. This is difficult to do; you may need to use a pair of pliers to apply a small amount of pressure to the acorn. Compare the parts of the nut from the acorn with the illustration of a lima bean seed. What similarities and differences do you notice? Caution: Do not taste the acorns or the nuts within them.

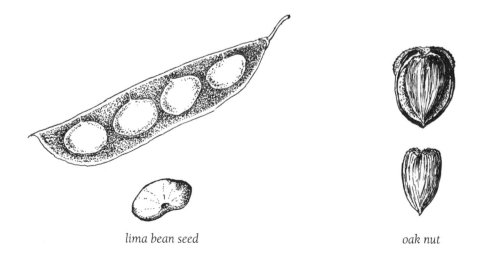

lima bean seed

oak nut

Plant an acorn as the squirrels do. Bury several acorns of the same type of oak in the soil. Water them, and dig one up at regular intervals to observe how they sprout. Keep a record of the changes that occur. (Don't be discouraged if your acorns don't sprout.)

Oak Twigs and Buds. Nothing can take the place of firsthand observations when it comes to learning about the complexities and varieties of twig structure. You will soon find that twigs come in a variety of shapes, sizes, colors, and textures. Examining bare twigs during the colder months will allow you to focus on the buds, the shape of the twigs, and their color and texture. You will notice that buds develop at the ends (terminal buds) and along the sides (lateral buds) of the twigs. The developing tissue in the terminal bud adds length to the twig. The lateral buds produce flowers, leaves, or new branches.

How many buds are there on the twig? Where are they located? How many are terminal buds? How many are side buds? Are they opposite each other on the twig or are they alternate, appearing stepped? How do the side buds resemble the terminal buds? Are the buds pointed or roundish? What is the texture? Are they smooth or hairy? Sticky?

Compare the oak twigs and buds you have found with the illustrations below.

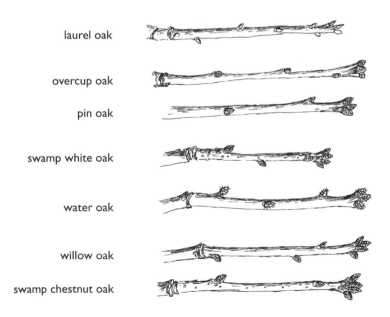

laurel oak

overcup oak

pin oak

swamp white oak

water oak

willow oak

swamp chestnut oak

Oak trees typically have clusters of buds at the ends of their twigs.

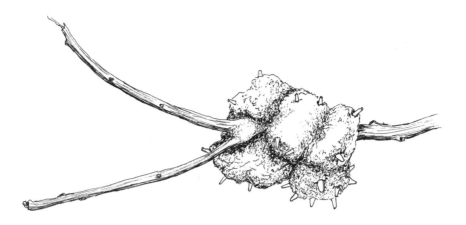

Horned oak galls protect the female wasp inside.

Galls. During the winter, when the oak trees are bare of leaves, you can see hundreds of small, dark, round shapes, larger than acorns but mostly smaller than golf balls, scattered through the small twigs at the outer edges of the trees. These are galls—woody growths produced by the tree as protective homes for immature insects. You may think the tree is generous to house these nurseries, but the story of galls and oaks is not a story of altruism, but of a cooperative arrangement between plants and insects.

There are over two thousand different kinds of galls in North America, and they live on all kinds of trees and plants, including oaks, hickories, willows, birches, roses, goldenrod, and daisies. On oak trees alone, there are eight hundred different kinds of galls.

The exact nature of gall formation is not yet known. It is known that insects secrete growth-regulating chemicals called auxins. In response to the auxins secreted by an egg-laying female or by the larva that develops from the egg, the plant either produces new cells or enlarges some existing cells. The result is a gall unique to the insect species that caused it.

Look for galls on the small twigs of oaks and other trees such as hickories, willows, birch, and poplars. Once you begin hunting for galls, you will be amazed at how easy they are to find. Examine some of the galls you find. Are they hard, woody, or some other consistency? Can you crush them with your hand? Are they round, oval, or some other shape? Do they have spines? How big are they? Assuming an insect caused the gall, can you find the exit holes the adult used to escape? How many holes are there? You might also find larger holes made by woodpeckers, which eat the larvae inside the galls.

The architecture inside galls is often very complex. To see some of this work, you need to open the galls. Some galls have a stem you can open with a fingernail or a penknife. Observe the inside of several galls. Do they have one large chamber or several? Make some drawings to illustrate the interior designs of the more elaborate galls you find. These would be good subjects for close-up photography. Are there any little grubs or other creatures living inside?

TREE GALLS

Tree	Location of the Gall	Appearance

At other times of the year, when the leaves are on the trees, you may find galls on oak leaves as well. Many of these have been formed by cynipid wasps, small insects that are seldom seen. Cynipid wasps belong to the order Hymenoptera, members of which are the cause of about one-third of all galls. Cynipid wasps produce horned oak galls—rounded brown balls with woody

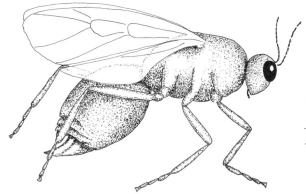

The cynipid wasp is just one of the many gall-causing wasps.

Life cycle of the horned oak gall

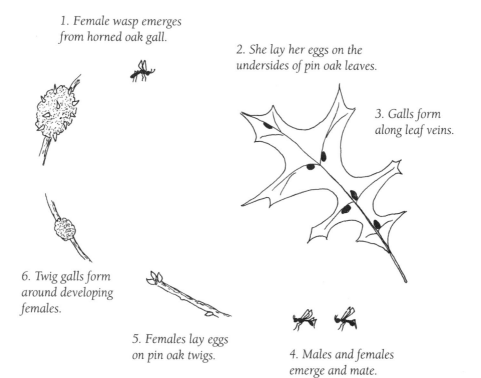

1. Female wasp emerges from horned oak gall.

2. She lay her eggs on the undersides of pin oak leaves.

3. Galls form along leaf veins.

6. Twig galls form around developing females.

5. Females lay eggs on pin oak twigs.

4. Males and females emerge and mate.

spikes—on twigs of pin and other red oaks. The woolsower gall, which has woolly filaments and appears on white oak, is caused by a gallfly, another member of the order Hymenoptera.

OTHER WETLAND TREES

Oak trees are not the only deciduous trees that flourish in wet places. In the activities that follow, you will have an opportunity to learn about other trees that grow in these habitats. Exploring these wetland trees will help you put oak trees into a broader picture. You will discover some interesting facts not only about the trees, but also about the wild things that depend on them for food and shelter. Record your observations in your notebook.

More About Leaves. A first step in getting to know trees is to become familiar with their leaves. Observe the leaves of wetland trees other than oaks. Ask the following questions about each kind of leaf: Is the leaf simple, with just one blade attached to the leaf stem, or compound, having several leaflets attached to the leaf stem? Is it heart shaped, oval, lance shaped, egg

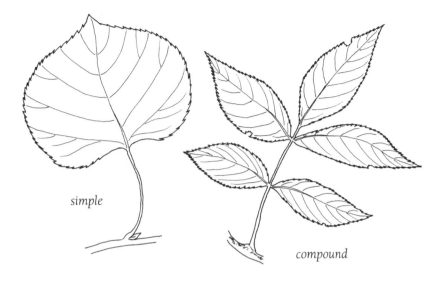

simple

compound

shaped, or somewhat triangular? Is the color or texture of the leaf the same or different on top and bottom surfaces? Does it feel fuzzy or smooth? Does it have lobes? Are the edges serrated (toothed), doubly serrated, smooth, or wavy? How are the leaves arranged on the twig? Are they opposite each other or are they alternately placed? Or are they whorled, radiating out like spokes from a wagon wheel? Which is the most common leaf arrangement on the trees in your sample?

Leaves on a twig are arranged in one of three patterns:

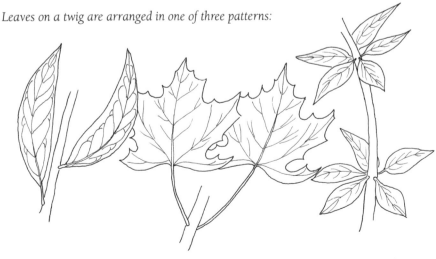

Alternate: a single leaf at each node.

Opposite: two leaves at each node.

Whorled: more than two leaves at each node.

The Trees

Red Maple (*Acer rubrum*). This is a common hardwood in swamps and other wet places, although it also grows at higher elevations. You will find this adaptable tree growing with black gum, larch, Atlantic white cedar, swamp white oak (*Q. bicolor*), speckled alder, and blueberry in the Northern Atlantic states. To the south, red maple grows with tupelo gum, bald cypress, and pin oak (*Q. palustris*).

Leaves. The leaves are simple, with three to five lobes, and a whitened green on the undersurface.

Twigs and buds. Twigs are slender and dark red to reddish brown, with small, rounded leaf buds that have overlapping scales. The buds appear opposite each other on the twig.

Black Ash (*Fraxinus nigra*). This medium-size tree does not tolerate shade but is comfortable in some standing water. It grows to about sixty-six feet and is found in association with tamarack, white cedar, eastern hemlock, and yellow birch. It flowers in the early spring, and fruits ripen by late summer. Wood ducks, grouse, turkeys, and many songbirds and small mammals eat the fruits, and white-tailed deer and moose browse on twigs and leaves.

Leaves. The leaves occur in pairs opposite each other on the twigs and branches. They are compound, with seven to eleven stalkless leaflets.

Twigs and buds. Twigs are stout, round, and dark green to gray. Buds appear in opposite pairs and are dark brown to nearly black and rounded. The terminal bud is larger than the lateral buds.

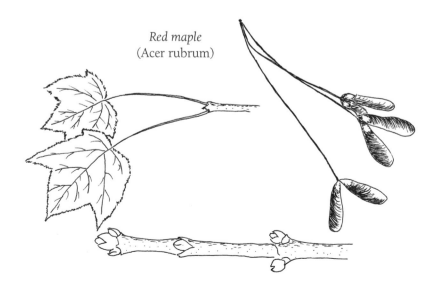

Red maple
(Acer rubrum)

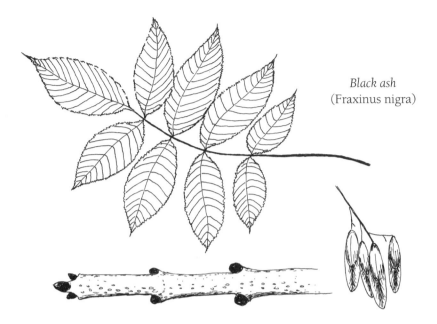

Black ash
(Fraxinus nigra)

Eastern Cottonwood (*Populus deltoides*). This tree favors moist lowlands, but you can also find it growing on moist, well-drained silty or sandy slopes. You may find it growing with sweet gum, sycamore, and several kinds of lowland oaks. It may reach 130 feet in thirty years. Beavers, squirrels, and porcupines eat the bark, leaves, and buds; deer and moose browse on twigs and leaves; and grouse and songbirds feed on the buds.

Leaves. The simple leaves occur alternately on the twigs. They are broad, somewhat triangular, and toothed along the edges.

Twigs and buds. Twigs are hairless and yellowish, turning bright or dark orange in the first year and becoming pale gray the second year. The terminal bud is sticky, long, and pointed.

Black Willow (*Salix nigra*). This willow, sometimes called swamp willow, can grow more than 130 feet high in its southern range, but to the north it grows to only half that height. This water-loving tree graces streambanks and river margins. You may find it in wet places such as swamps and along gullies and drainage ditches, in association with cottonwood, river birch, black spruce, water tupelo, and bald cypress. Deer and rodents nibble on the shoots, and sapsuckers feed on the sap in wells they excavate from the inner bark.

Leaves. The thin, papery, light green leaves appear alternately on the twigs. They are lance shaped, finely toothed along the edges, and three to six inches in length.

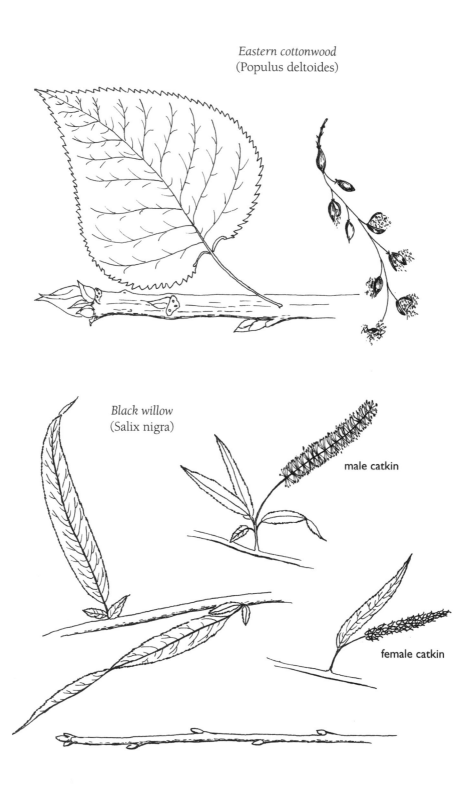

Eastern cottonwood
(Populus deltoides)

Black willow
(Salix nigra)

male catkin

female catkin

Twigs and buds. Twigs are long and limp. They may be reddish olive or reddish with the tip bright orange or red. Pendulous flowers called catkins grow at the tips of leafy branchlets. Male and female catkins grow on separate trees. Tannish buds are ⅛ to ¼ inch long and are capped by a single scale.

Eastern Sycamore (*Platanus occidentalis*). This tree tolerates very wet, poorly drained soils. It may grow in clusters along streambanks, but most frequently it is found in the company of red maple, sweet gum, willow, silver maple, cottonwood, and box elder. Deer and muskrats eat the twigs, and small rodents feed on fallen seeds. Tree cavities provide nesting spaces and shelter for wood ducks, raccoons, and opossums.

Leaves. The leaves have three to five lobes, are hairless, and have large teeth along the margin. The base of each leaf covers the next year's bud.

Twigs and buds. When young, the twigs are dark green and covered with fine hairs. As they mature, they become orange-brown, smooth, and shiny. Buds along the sides of the twigs are cone-shaped, covered by three smooth and shiny scales. There are generally no buds at the end of the twigs.

Bark. The bark of the sycamore is unique. When mature, it falls off in large, irregular patches, exposing the yellow or white underbark.

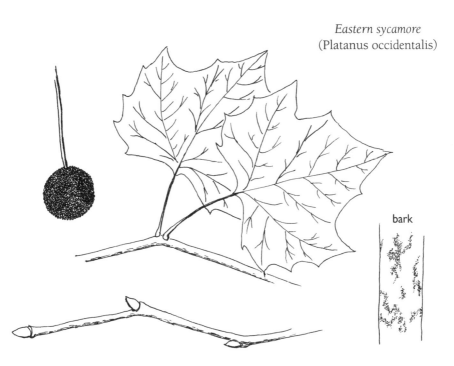

Eastern sycamore
(Platanus occidentalis)

bark

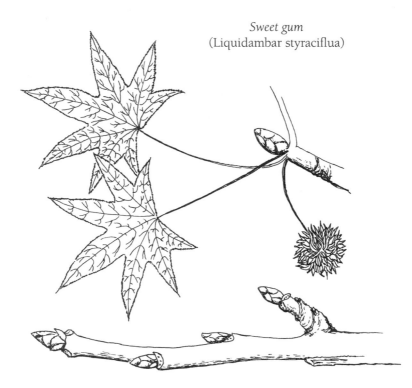

Sweet gum
(Liquidambar styraciflua)

Sweet Gum (*Liquidambar styraciflua*). This tree can be found in poorly drained soils and swamp lands, where it grows along with bald cypress, willow oak, and pin oak.

Leaves. The light green leaves are star shaped with pointed tips and square at the base. They give off a pleasant fragrance when crushed. Songbirds, wild turkeys, chipmunks, and gray squirrels eat the seeds.

Twigs and buds. The twigs are slender and light orange, becoming reddish brown with age. Leaf scars are prominent. Cone-shaped buds are pointed at the tip and covered with shiny, reddish-brown scales.

CHAPTER 3

Cattails

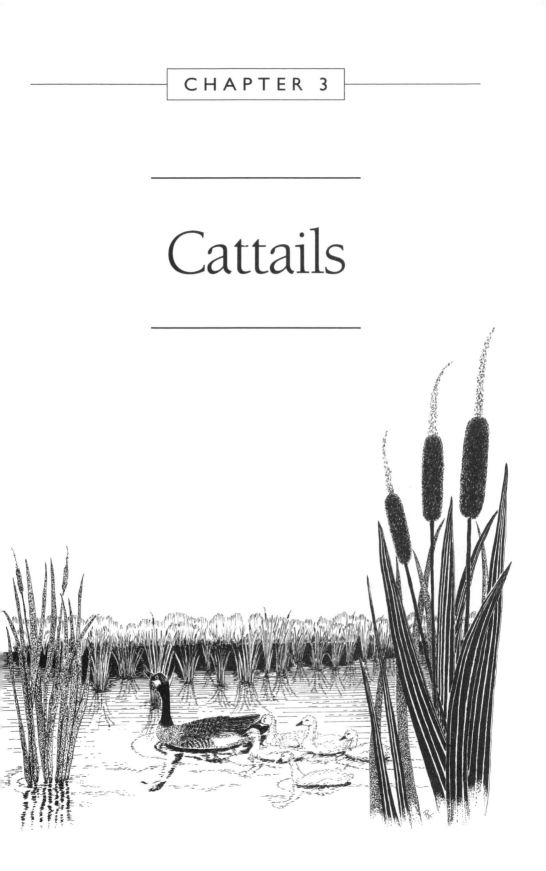

CIGARS AND YELLOW SMOKE

The damp cold of winter lingers in the air, and the calendar tells us that spring has not officially arrived, yet the unmistakable spring wake-up call is heard from the marsh. The *konk-a-lee* of male red-winged blackbirds signals their return from southern wintering grounds. Because flocks of females will soon join them, the males are busy marking territories in preparation for the business of courting and mating. These spring songsters can hold our attention so well that we may miss seeing their stage, the dry remains of last year's cattails.

Cattails are familiar to many of us. But like so many things that are in the background, we don't give them much thought. These tall, slender-leaved plants with brown, velveteen, cigarlike spikes grow in marshy places along highways, at the rim of ponds and potholes, in roadside ditches, and in other wet places. During the winter months, the furry beige interior spills out, making the spikes resemble sheep in need of shearing.

Cattails are emergent plants of the wetlands. This means that they are rooted in shallow water and their tops grow out of the water—they emerge into the air. Several characteristics make life in marshy land possible for them. Even though the waterlogged soil where they grow is low in oxygen content, cattails find the conditions satisfactory. They can tolerate standing in water from six to twelve inches deep, which their landlocked neighbors, the sedges, would find unsatisfactory. A lush system of fine, fibrous roots easily threads its way through the ooze and firmly anchors the plant in place. Unbranched, reedlike stems grow from three to nine feet tall and support the male and female flower spikes that you see in late spring. Straight, narrow, olive-green leaves, often shorter than the stem they flank, are often the first sign of renewed growth each spring. You can observe this as the growing season begins in your area.

Cattails have developed two reproductive strategies that make them highly successful colonizers of wet areas. One strategy involves the plant and its system of underground stems, called rhizomes. Rhizomes generally grow horizontally, parallel to the surface of the soil and only a few inches below it. Although new shoots develop from the rhizomes in the cool of the autumn, growth ceases in the cold temperatures of winter, and it is not until the warm days of early spring that the growth process resumes.

Because this method of reproduction does not involve the union of sex cells from two different parents, it is called asexual. The new plants that develop are genetically identical to the parent plant and are called clones. The

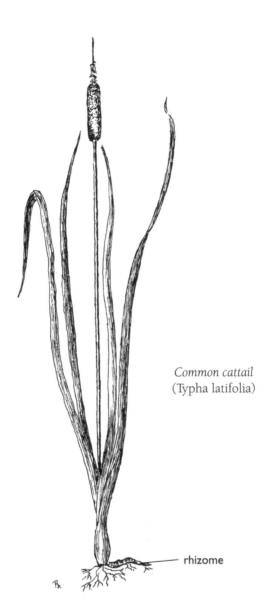

Common cattail
(Typha latifolia)

rhizome

clones and the parent plant form a cluster and can be considered one plant. The advantage of this arrangement is that the plant can survive much longer than any of the individual stems that make up the group. These clonal clusters of cattails become so intertwined that it is nearly impossible to identify separate clonal stands without digging up the entire rhizome system, which can become quite large. Scientists documented one rhizome system that yielded one hundred clones in a year, in a ten-foot-diameter cluster.

It's interesting to note that goldenrod also reproduces asexually through a similar system and produces clonal groups. Individual members of these groups are much easier to identify, because they do not form densely packed clonal clusters like the cattails. Look for their circular clusters in fields and meadows throughout the summer months.

The other method of cattail reproduction yields seeds, which develop from the union of male and female sex cells, called gametes. If you look at a cattail in June or early July, you will notice that the upper half of the flower spike is covered with a massive amount of yellow powder. The tiny particles that make up the powder are pollen grains, which are male sex cells. When mature, the tiny pollen grains are carried away from the spike that produced

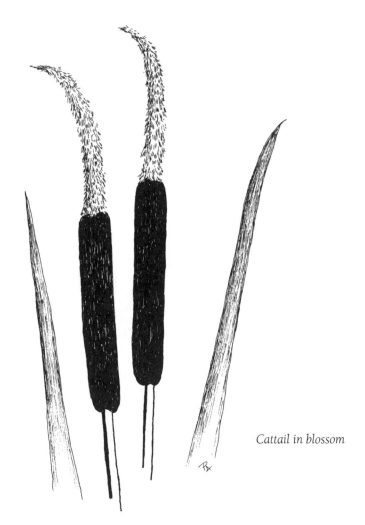

Cattail in blossom

THE PLAYERS

them by the slightest breeze. Sometimes you may see dense puffs of "yellow smoke" rising from pollen-producing portions of the cattail spike. Soon after the pollen is dispersed, the male flower spikes die and drop off.

Meanwhile, female flowers are developing on the lower half of the spike. After the flowers are fertilized by the pollen, the plant produces a profusion of downy seeds; some estimates are as high as two hundred thousand seeds per female spike. The fluffy mass continues to swell and release its fruits throughout the winter. The seeds, equipped with plumes of silk, are dispersed by the wind to less populated areas away from the parent plant. This strategy provides the opportunity for seeds to germinate in places where there is minimal competition for space and light. Although the seed-germinated cattails do not produce flowers until their second year, rhizome growth and development begin during the first year. One rhizome yielded a ten-foot-wide clonal cluster the first year. This underground activity is another reason why seed-grown plants are considered cattail pioneers that can thrive in previously uncolonized marshy areas.

When cattails complete their reproductive cycle, they wither, die, and become part of the organic litter that falls onto the black ooze that makes up the wetland soil. Bacteria eventually reduce this material to its elemental forms, and the nutrients released by the process are made available to the wetland system. As plant litter continues to accumulate, the nature of the wetland gradually changes from marsh to dry meadow. Over a period of many decades, the soggy ground that nourished the cattails becomes drier, and eventually wildflowers and then woody shrubs such as alders and willows, as well as other plants that prefer drier surroundings, begin to grow here.

In general, cattails do not offer much in the way of food for wildlife, although moose, elk, and muskrats nibble on the green shoots when they first appear in the spring. Geese also favor the tender young shoots, as well as the starchy underground roots. Although the seeds are too small to be of nutrient value for most birds, you may see small birds pecking at the shaggy spikes during the winter. These birds, in need of high-energy food, are digging for the nutrient-rich moth larvae that overwinter in the cattail seed heads.

In earlier days, Native Americans ate the carbohydrate-rich roots and lower portion of young stems for the quick energy they provided. They also roasted the immature flower spikes and ate them like corn on the cob. Mature pollen from the male flower stalk made a protein-rich flour that, mixed with wheat flour, provided a nourishing base for breads, hotcakes, and other baked goods. Today, cattail leaves are used for woven chair seats and backs, as well as rugs and mats.

OBSERVATIONS

Cattails are widely distributed throughout the wetlands of North America. Close-growing stands of cattails often prevent the growth of other plants that would compete with them for water, sunlight, and nutrients. As a result, you will not find a profusion of other wetland plants growing among dense thickets of cattail stalks. When cattails grow in more open stands, ferns, sedges, and other plants that thrive in soggy soils are also part of the community.

The primary nonplant residents of a cattail community are the many species of spiders, insects, fish, turtles, birds, and mammals that find food and shelter there. You will have an opportunity to learn about these residents in some of the activities below.

Types of Cattails. There are two different types of cattails. You can easily identify the broad-leaved cattail (*Typha latifolia*) by the arrangement of the flower spikes. The yellowish male (pistillate) flower spike is directly above the stout, brown cylinder of the female (staminate) flowers. This cattail grows in water depths of six inches to two feet. It has a low tolerance for pollution, and it grows robustly in acidic soil.

A close cousin is the narrow-leaved cattail (*Typha angustifolia*). The most obvious distinction between this and the broad-leaved cattail is the conspicuous space that separates the male and female flower spikes in the narrow-leaved cattail. Also, as its name implies, the straplike leaves of this cattail are more slender. Although the two species live in the same marshes and ponds, the narrow-leaved cattail is less widely distributed and grows in deeper water of three feet or more. Their close association often produces hybrids, which can make identification difficult. The narrow-leaved cattail is more tolerant of pollution and grows well in waters steeped in fertilizer runoff.

Find a cattail growing in a roadside ditch, close to a pond, or in a wetland. Draw a picture or take a photograph of it. Determine whether you are looking at a broad-leaved or a narrow-leaved cattail. First, look for the male and female flower spikes. Are they touching each other or is there a gap between them? If there is a gap, how wide is it?

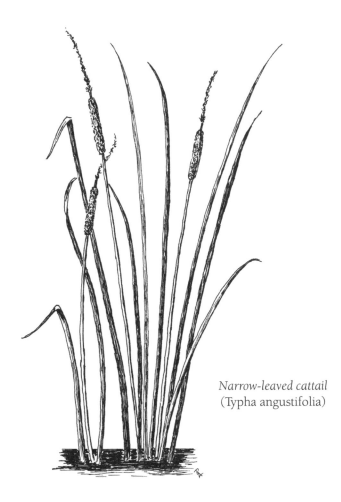

Narrow-leaved cattail
(Typha angustifolia)

Next, measure the leaves. How wide are they? Do they taper? Are they uniformly thick throughout their entire length? Examine the leaf from tip to base. Is it flexible at the base where it clasps the stem? Describe the texture of the leaf. Where on the leaf would you expect to find wind damage when it occurs?

Cattail Habitat. Where are cattails found in your area? If there are no nearby marshes or bodies of water, look for them in roadside ditches and along highways from your car. Write a description of the place where you find them. Are they near a pond, a pothole, or in a ditch? How far inland from water are they growing? Is the land on which they grow underwater through-out the year or for any part of the year, or is the land dry throughout the year? Is the cattail zone sharply defined by wet soil on one side and dry soil on the other side? How big is the area where the cattails are growing?

Wetland Companions. While you are looking for cattails, you will find other plants growing in the area.

Rushes. Grasslike rushes have round, often hollow stems. Look for seeds on the sides of the stems close to the top. There are several types of rushes, among them spike rush and soft rush, sometimes called bog rush.

Sedges. Remembering that "sedges have edges" is an easy way for beginners to learn to identify these plants. If you cut a sedge stem crosswise and look at it with a hand lens, you will see the triangular shape that gives the stem its edges. You are likely to find tussock sedge and bulrush in wet places.

Grasses. An identifying feature of grasses is their hollow, cylindrical, and jointed stems. Their leaves are attached at the joints. Look at the grass growing in your yard to see these features that distinguish grasses from sedges and rushes.

Cattails Through the Seasons. Follow the cattails you found through the year, recording in your notebook your observations and the dates you made them. Make sketches or take photographs of the changes that occur. Note such things as when the pollen matures and begins to drift away from the male flower spike, when the fluffy seeds make their appearance on the female flower spike, how long the seeds persist on the flower stalk, and when the green color of the growing season gives way to the tans and beiges of autumn.

Look for dead cattail stems, leaves, and spikes jutting above the snow and ice along the edges of ditches and ponds and along the highways. What happens to them in the spring?

Seeds. Cattails are prodigious producers of seeds. Some estimates exceed two hundred thousand seeds from a single flower stalk. To get an idea of how compactly the seeds are packed on the stalk, find a fluffy cattail and pull off a pinch of the brown felt. Rest the clump in the palm of your hand and watch what happens. Try this on different days to see whether the temperature affects the rate at which it occurs. Write down the temperature on each try and the time it took for the clump to open. Is the reaction faster on a warm day than on a cold day? What are the implications of this for seed dispersal?

Many cattail flower spikes that remain on the stalk throughout the winter appear shaggy. This appearance begins as hundreds of thousands of tiny seeds loosen from the central flower spikes. Collect a few cattail seeds and, with the help of a hand lens, make a drawing of one. How do these seeds, with their silken threads, compare with the seeds of dandelion or thistle?

Leaves. How are the leaves arranged on the plant? Are they arranged opposite or alternately? Remove a leaf from one plant. What is its shape? How

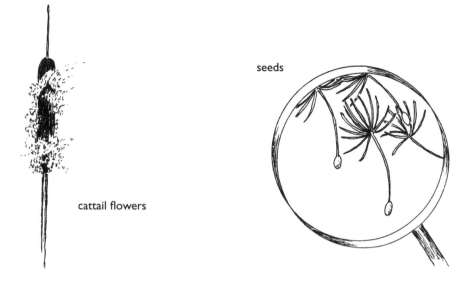

seeds

cattail flowers

Throughout the winter, cattail flower spikes break apart. Wind and water disperse the seeds to new areas.

does the leaf differ along its length? Where is it widest? Is the color constant along the entire length of the leaf? How would you explain your observation? Describe the texture. How far can you bend the leaf before it begins to break?

Describe the attachment of the leaf to the base of the plant. Is each leaf attached in the same way to the base? Where is the leaf the stiffest or toughest? Where is it the most pliable or bendable? Explain the advantage of this arrangement to the top-heavy stalk in strong winds. Do any leaves look as though they have been damaged by wind?

Cut across a leaf near where it joins the main stalk, and also near its tip. With the help of a hand lens, look at the cross sections to see how the leaf is veined. Make a drawing of what you see. What made the leaf so difficult to cut?

Split the leaf lengthwise. What other supports do you see in the leaf? Try tearing or breaking the leaf along its edges. Can you find any signs of wind damage?

Use a small, sharp knife to peel back the green covering on the leaf. This will give you another view of the leaf's latticework structural support. Like the struts of an airplane wing, this support helps keep the slender, vertical leaf from falling over.

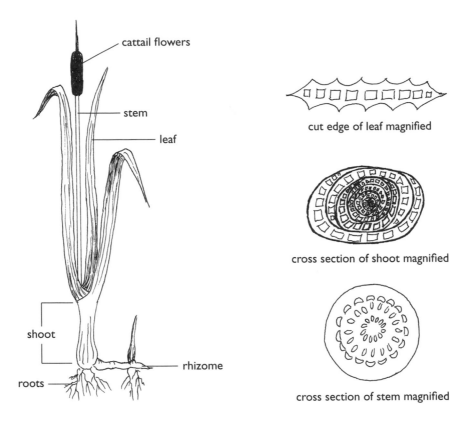

cattail flowers

stem

leaf

shoot

roots

rhizome

cut edge of leaf magnified

cross section of shoot magnified

cross section of stem magnified

Wetland Communities. Many different kinds of birds, fish, reptiles, amphibians, mammals, insects, and spiders have established communities among these wetland plants.

Birds. Many wetland birds find that dead cattail stalks and leaves make suitable nest material and that the seclusion of the wetland provides reasonable safety for them and their young. A good time to see their nests is during the late fall and winter, when your view is not blocked by vegetation and you will not disturb nesting birds. Songbirds such as red-winged blackbirds, marsh wrens, and swamp sparrows build nests suspended in the stalks away from the water's edge, several feet above the water level and wet soil. Wetland birds such as grebes, sora rails, Virginia rails, mute swans, least bitterns, American coots, and ducks find suitable nesting material among the cattails. Look for their platform nests close to the water's edge.

Fish. Bottom-feeding fish such as carp poke around at the base of cattails. In ponds, especially in sunny areas, you may find sunfish, bluegills, pumpkinseeds, or black crappie, which swim along weedy shorelines.

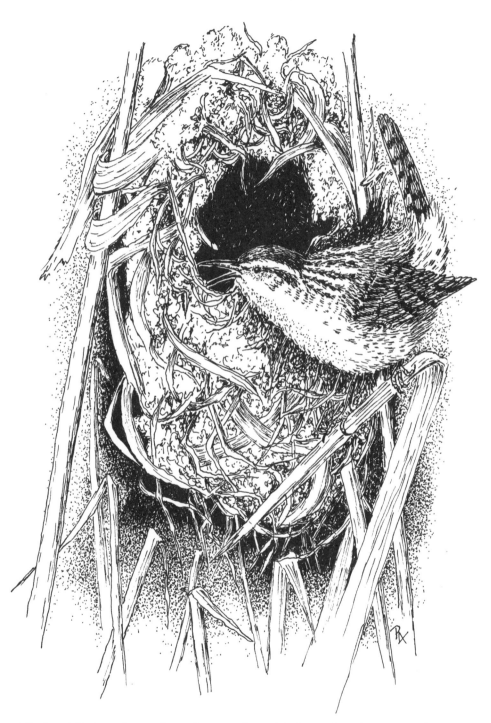

The long-billed marsh wren (Cistothorus palustris) *lashes its domed nest to standing cattails. The nest is woven of wet cattails, reeds, grasses, and cattail down.*

CATTAILS

Reptiles. Eastern painted turtles, mud turtles, spotted turtles, and snapping turtles may be found in ponds, pools, roadside ditches, and other wet places. Turtles are primarily scavengers, but the painted turtles are known to eat cattail stems.

Amphibians. Green frogs, bullfrogs, leopard frogs, pickerel frogs, and spring peepers are annual visitors to ponds and pools. Pairs mate, the females lay their eggs, and the tadpoles develop in these and other wet places. The red-spotted newt is another common resident in ponds and pools. This is the aquatic adult stage of the land-based red eft, which roams the forest floor. The newt feeds on the eggs of other amphibians, including frogs.

Mammals. Cattails provide food for muskrats, as well as building materials for their lodges. These wetland mammals are gregarious, and when you see one, there are usually many more in the area. Muskrats produce as many as three litters a year.

Insects. Cattails are populated by many different kinds of insects, including sap-drinking aphids and the cattail mosquito. Several moths belonging to the Noctuidae family may be found in cattail habitat. The larvae, or caterpillars, of the developing moths make their living as leaf miners, and they find the long, flat leaves of cattails especially desirable.

After hatching from eggs laid on the leaf, the minute larvae make holes in the skin of the leaf and crawl inside. If you study a leaf carefully, you will find that it has an upper and a lower skin, with additional layers inside the leaf. One of these middle layers is called the spongy mesophyll. Many leaf miners dwell in this spongelike layer and eat their way through it, removing the chlorophyll-containing cells. What remains are the transparent upper and lower surfaces of the leaf, and the mines show up as tan squiggled lines or blotches on the leaf surfaces. Frequently, you can see the flattened bodies of leaf miners, a physical adaptation to the cramped quarters in which they live.

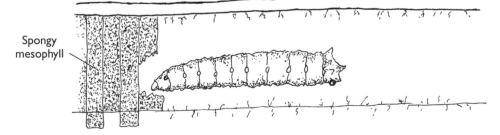

Spongy
mesophyll

This cross section of a leaf shows the damage caused by the developing leaf miner.

The black-and-yellow argiope spider often spins its orb-shaped web among cattails.

In their snug homes, the larvae mature into adults, leave the mines, mate and reproduce, and the cycle begins again. Look for the mines of these caterpillars as you explore the world of cattails.

Spiders. Sac spiders (family Clubionidae) build incubation chambers for their eggs by folding down the tips of cattail leaves and sewing the fold to form envelopes. The female spiders lay their eggs in the envelopes, where they remain to become the first food for the hatchlings. Look for these envelopes on cattail leaves. At what time of the year do you see them?

Another spider that lives among the cattails is the black-and-yellow argiope (*Argiope aurantia*). This spider builds a large, vertical, orb-shaped web. Look for these webs among cattails. At what time of the year do you find them?

CHAPTER 4

Ferns

SUCCESS STORY

When you first walk into the forest on a hot summer day, you are relieved to feel the cool, moist shade. As you walk along the path, you notice the small trees and bushes that thrive in the sun-mottled shade, as well as dense patches of ferns. Ferns are especially abundant in the wet areas near streams.

These common woodland plants have an exotic, ancient aura to them, like prehistoric relics. Ferns and their close relatives actually did flourish in the steamy forests of the dinosaur ages in the Carboniferous period, about 350 million years ago. The stable climate of that time encouraged their growth. Flat, marshy land and vast inland seas contributed to the success of these early land-dwelling plants. The forests of ferns they created flourished over a large portion of the earth, including what are now the icy polar regions. The cooling climate that followed this period resulted in the evolution of the ferns we see today, which are adapted to changing sets of environmental conditions. Today there are some twelve thousand fern species, about four hundred of which live in the United States, and about one hundred of those in the Northeast. Ferns of various sizes and shapes live in a diversity of habitats, ranging from tropical rain forests to the arctic tundra. Robust, eighty-foot-tall fern trees thrive in the tropics, and dainty, two-inch leaves of curly grass fern (*Schizaea pusilla*) grow in the acid soils of southern New Jersey bogs. You also can find ferns in such unlikely places as the marshlands of northern Alaska and even Antarctica. However, few grow in arid deserts.

Ferns were the first plants with vascular systems. These systems carry minerals and water to the food factories in the leaves and the manufactured nutrients from the leaves to all parts of the plant. They also provide support so that these plants can stand upright.

Ancient mythology often attributed magical qualities to ferns. People noticed that ferns did not possess obvious structures related to reproduction, such as flowers, fruits, and seeds, but the plants continued to appear year after year. Compared with other plants, the ferns were a strange anomaly.

A rudimentary understanding of how ferns reproduce dates back only three hundred years, to 1669, when spores were discovered. But at that time, scientists were unable to make the connection between these tiny structures and fern reproduction. It was not until the mid-eighteenth century that this relationship became clear. However, the scientific explanation itself is quite an intricate tale filled with strange terminology.

Spores are tiny cells that do not contain a baby plant or embryo. Therefore, spores do not become new ferns, but if they fall on suitable soil and have adequate water, they will divide and produce a tiny structure called a prothallium

Life cycle of ferns

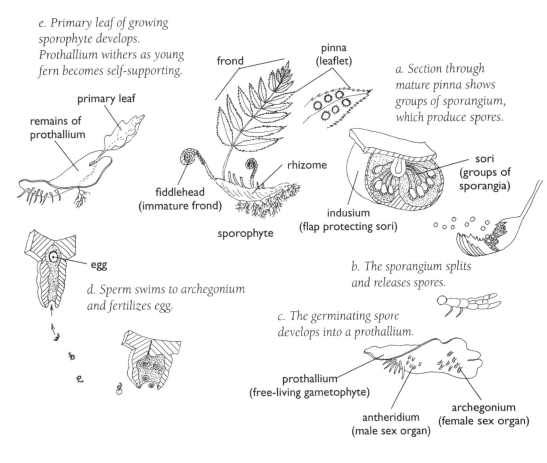

e. Primary leaf of growing sporophyte develops. Prothallium withers as young fern becomes self-supporting.

primary leaf

remains of prothallium

frond

pinna (leaflet)

a. Section through mature pinna shows groups of sporangium, which produce spores.

fiddlehead (immature frond)

rhizome

sporophyte

sori (groups of sporangia)

indusium (flap protecting sori)

egg

d. Sperm swims to archegonium and fertilizes egg.

b. The sporangium splits and releases spores.

c. The germinating spore develops into a prothallium.

prothallium (free-living gametophyte)

antheridium (male sex organ)

archegonium (female sex organ)

(plural, prothallia). These flat, often heart-shaped structures lack leaves, stems, roots, and vascular systems. Prothallia get their nutrients directly from the surrounding water, which doesn't have to be more than a thin film over the ground. The prothallia are small, growing only to about one-fourth inch in diameter, and are only about one cell thick except near the center. In this slightly thicker region, on the underside, two small structures develop. One of these is the archegonium, which contains an egg, and the other is the antheridium, which contains antherozoids or sperm. Spores need moisture for fertilization to take place, as the antherozoids must swim to the archegonium. The fertilized egg that develops from this union eventually becomes the plant we recognize as the fern. During this development, the prothallium withers, and the young fern becomes self-supporting. Often referred to as the

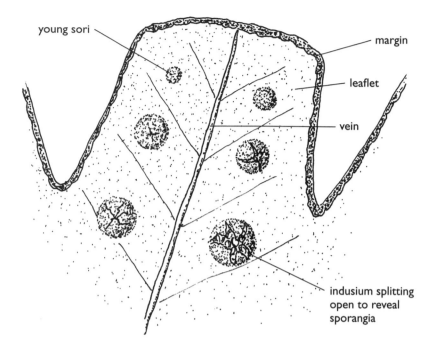

young sori

margin

leaflet

vein

indusium splitting
open to reveal
sporangia

private life of the fern, this phase in the two-part life cycle of a fern is called the gametophyte generation.

The self-supporting fernlets have tightly coiled, bright green heads, called crosiers, or fiddleheads, which poke their way through the soil in the spring. As the fern matures, the coils straighten into leaves, or fronds. With the unfurling of its young fronds, the fern enters another stage of its life cycle. Now its job is to produce spores. Some ferns produce hundreds of thousands of spores, and other, more prodigious ferns produce millions.

Individual fern species have their own unique patterns of spore production, but generalizations about this process can be made. In the spring, tiny green bumps appear on the undersides of the leaves. As the season progresses toward summer, these bumps turn brown, and the leaves may look as though they are growing fungi. These dark brown spots are called sori, and they contain spore cases, or sporangia. Sometimes the sporangia are covered with a thin protective membrane called an indusium.

When the spores are mature, they are released from the sporangium. The method of release varies among species. In some ferns, the spores are shot into the air by a slingshot-like mechanism. In other species, the spore cases simply open, and the spores are caught in air currents and drift away from the parent fern. Whatever the discharge mechanism, the spores of all ferns become airborne with the slightest breeze, even by an imperceptible movement of air.

Relatively few spores come to rest on suitable soil. Those that land in warm, shady, moist places at the right time of year will begin to grow. If conditions are not appropriate at the time of their landing, the spores remain alive but inactive for as long as a year. This spore-producing phase in the life cycle of a fern is called the sporophyte generation.

The complete life cycle of a fern is even much more complicated than has been outlined here. If you keep in mind the following, however, you can easily remember the essential steps in the cycle: 1. Fronds produce spores. 2. Spores develop into prothallia. 3. Prothallia manufacture gametes. 4. Gametes fuse to produce a new fern (the sporophyte). In the activity section, you will have an opportunity to explore this process in some specific ferns.

This pattern of shifting between asexual and sexual development is known as alternation of generations. Although it is the usual pattern of fern reproduction, not all ferns are restricted to it; some can reproduce vegetatively as well. One way they do this is by the branching and rebranching of their rhizomes (a special type of stem). Some ferns send out a "feeler" rhizome that roots some distance from the parent fern. When this happens, a new population of ferns appears where there were none before.

Ferns also can reproduce asexually by vegetative reproduction of fronds, roots, or rhizomes. This method does not use spores or require the union of gametes, and the offspring are identical copies, or clones, of the parent plant. As long as the habitat conditions meet the requirements of the parent plants, the clones and resulting population will survive.

The rare walking fern (*Camptosorus rhizophyllus*) demonstrates a form of vegetative reproduction. Its long, lance-shaped fronds arch away from the center of the plant. When the tips of the fronds touch the earth, they produce roots and new plants. Because the new plant was not produced through the union of gametes or sex cells, it is a clone of its parent.

The Boston fern (*Nephrolepis exaltata bostoniensis*), used frequently as an interior decoration, reproduces vegetatively through the use of runners, string-like leafless stems that develop among the fronds. These runners will sprout roots wherever they touch soil.

Buds on the roots of the staghorn fern (*Platycerium* sp.) develop into fernlets. Some less familiar ferns develop clones on the upper surfaces of their fronds. Eventually the new ferns will leave the parent fern, develop roots and rhizomes, and become independent ferns.

Most ferns are perennials. When it turns cold at the end of the growing season, the fronds of these ferns turn brown and become brittle. Their life above the ground is over, but the rhizomes continue to live throughout the winter. When spring arrives, new shoots will sprout from the rhizomes. If you feel around a clump of ferns in the autumn, you may feel some hard, round forms. These are the beginnings of the fiddleheads that will appear next spring.

Some ferns are evergreen and, along with pines, cedars, and hollies, provide a splash of color to the winter landscape. The common Christmas fern (*Polystichum acrostichoides*), which gets its name from the eared, stocking-shaped lobes of its fronds, is an evergreen fern you might find along wooded sloping streambanks, near stone walls, and in rocky, wooded areas. The marginal wood fern (*Dryopteris marginalis*) and the rare hairy lipfern (*Cheilanthes lanosa*) are frequent members of the rocky slope community.

Wherever they grow, ferns lend a subtle feeling of wildness to their habitat. Compared with the cheery spring blooms of wildflowers, ferns are subdued and are easily ignored. However, there is great diversity and beauty to be found. Find some ferns. Make a commitment to spend a season with them, observe them, ask questions, and learn what they have to tell you. They might just develop into a lifelong passion. The activities that follow will help give you a new and rich perspective on these fascinating plants.

THE WORLD OF FERNS

What you will need
basic kit

Science skills
observing
comparing
recording
inferring

OBSERVATIONS

In the activities below, you will discover a world of plants very different from the flowering plants of fields and gardens. On ferns, you will not find the familiar flowers, fruits, and seeds. Instead, fronds, sporangia, and prothallia will be your new companions as you navigate through this complex yet beautiful world. The ferns you will examine in these activities are not restricted to wetland habitats, but are common and easily found. Use the diagram below to help familiarize yourself with some fern anatomy and the vocabulary that goes with it.

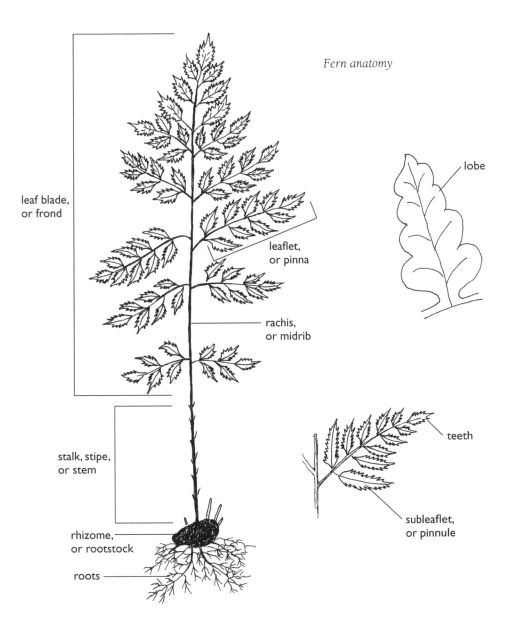

Fern anatomy

leaf blade, or frond

leaflet, or pinna

rachis, or midrib

stalk, stipe, or stem

rhizome, or rootstock

roots

lobe

teeth

subleaflet, or pinnule

Parts of a Fern

Frond, or Leaf Blade. The flat, green leaf blades, or fronds, the most conspicuous part of the fern, vary in size and shape. Fronds are usually compound, with leaflets, or pinnae, attached along a rachis, or midrib. The fronds manufacture food through photosynthesis. Some species have sterile and fertile leaves of different sizes and shapes. Fertile fronds contain reproductive spores. Fronds vary in size and shape in different species.

Stipe, or Stalk. The stipe, or stalk, is the leaf support below the rachis and above the root. It is covered with hairs or scales, rounded in back and concave or flat in front, and green, brown, tan, silver, or black in color.

Rachis. The rachis is the backbone of the frond and is the continuation of the stalk supporting the leaflets. It corresponds to the midrib of a simple leaf. Until the lobes in a fern are cut to the midrib, there is no rachis.

Leaflet, or Pinna (Plural, Pinnae). Leaflets are divisions of a compound leaf.

Subleaflet, or Pinnule. Subleaflets are subdivisions of leaflets.

Lobe, or Pinnulet. Lobes are the subdivision of a pinnule.

Teeth. Teeth are serrations along the edges of the pinnae, pinnules, or pinnulets.

Rhizome. Rhizomes are horizontal stems that lie on the surface of the soil or just below it.

Roots. Roots are thin, threadlike, sometimes wiry structures that anchor the plant and absorb water and minerals from the soil. They grow from the rootstock, or rhizomes.

Fern Identification. The shape of a frond will help you identify an unfamiliar fern. Is the frond triangular and broadest at the base, does it become narrow at both ends, or is it tapered only at the base?

 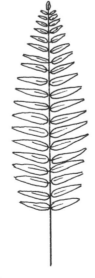 

a. broadest at base   b. semitapered at base   c. tapered to the base

Frond shapes

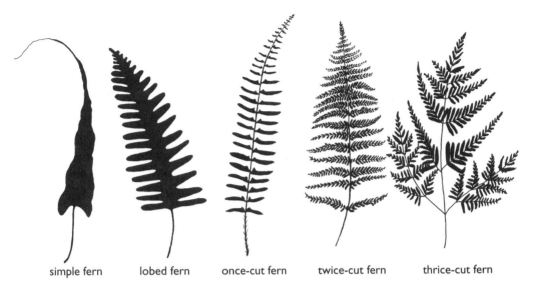

| simple fern | lobed fern | once-cut fern | twice-cut fern | thrice-cut fern |

Fronds come in many shapes and may be undivided, somewhat divided, or much divided into smaller parts.

Ferns vary in appearance. Some are extremely delicate; others are more substantial. There are differences in the lobes, leaflets, and subleaflets. Ferns are organized into groups having similar leaf patterns, which makes fern identification somewhat easier. Botanists who specialize in ferns use an even more detailed system than the one presented here to help them categorize these beauties.

Undivided Ferns. These ferns are very unlike the typical fern. The simple leaves are straplike and lack the feathery appearance of most ferns. These include the rare walking fern and the bird's nest fern *(Asplenium nidus)*, often grown as a houseplant.

Simple Ferns, or Lobed Ferns. Fronds of these ferns are divided by cuts on either side of the midrib but do not touch the midrib. The common polypody *(Polypodium virginianum)* has this design.

Compound Ferns. These ferns are cut into distinct leaflets to the midrib.

Once-cut ferns. Each leaflet, or pinna, is cut to the midrib. Ferns in this group are the sensitive fern *(Onoclea sensibilis)* and Christmas fern.

Twice-cut ferns. In these ferns, not only are the fronds cut into leaflets, but the leaflets are also cut into subleaflets, or pinnules. They include the marsh fern *(Thelypteris palustris)*, cinnamon fern *(Osmunda cinnemomea)*, ostrich fern *(Matteuccia struthiopteris)*, and marginal wood fern.

Thrice-cut ferns. In these, the laciest of ferns, the fronds are cut into leaflets (pinnae), which are cut into subleaflets (pinnules), which are cut again into pinnuletes. The common bracken fern *(Pteridium aquilinum)* of open fields and woods and the lady fern *(Athyrium filix-femina)* of moist, shaded woods are thrice-cut ferns.

Unfernlike Ferns. There are a few rare ferns that, in spite of their unfernlike appearance, are classified as ferns because they are vascular plants that reproduce by spores rather than seeds. The walking fern *(Camptosorus rhizophyllus)* prefers the northern face of moist limestone outcrops. The Hartford climbing fern *(Lygodium palmatum)* has vinelike fronds that climb and twist over shrubs and other obstacles in the partial or deep shade of low thickets and along streambanks in moist, wet, acid soil. It prefers sun, but the rhizomes must be wet. Curly grass fern *(Schizaea pusilla)* grows in wet, very acid soil, such as that found in cranberry bogs and cedar swamps. It is found in New Jersey, Nova Scotia, and Newfoundland.

Walking fern
(Camptosorus rhizophyllus)

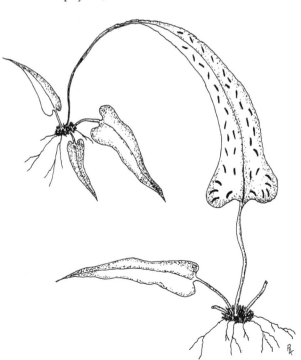

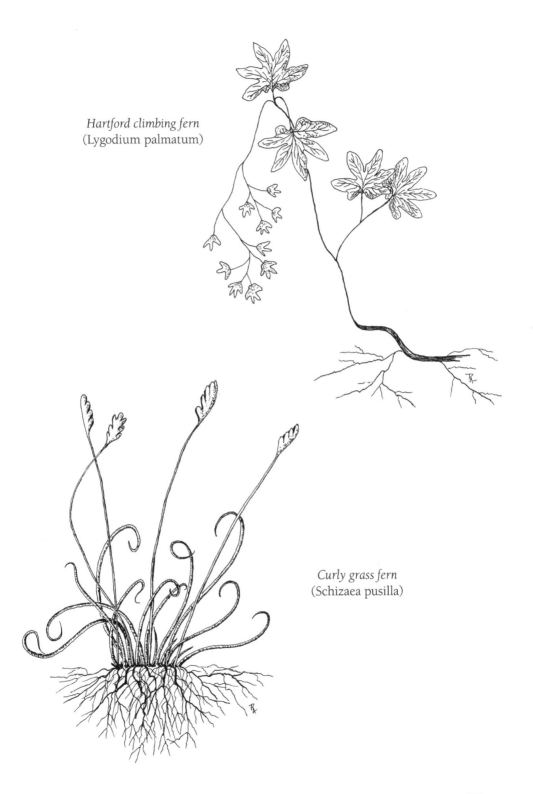

Hartford climbing fern
(Lygodium palmatum)

Curly grass fern
(Schizaea pusilla)

Finding Ferns. Ferns are easier to find than you might think. You will find them in moist, shaded areas, along riverbanks, around ponds, and in the woods. Here are brief descriptions of three common ferns you are likely to find growing in swampy areas and in wet woodlands.

The cinnamon fern has twice-cut fronds and a separate cinnamon-colored fertile frond growing from the rhizome that bears club-shaped sporangia. The tall, pointed sterile fronds grow in a circular pattern.

The ostrich fern has tall, plumelike, twice-cut sterile fronds that are wider in the middle and taper toward the base and the top of the frond. The fertile frond is also plume shaped, and its tough pinnae clasp dark brown clusters of sori.

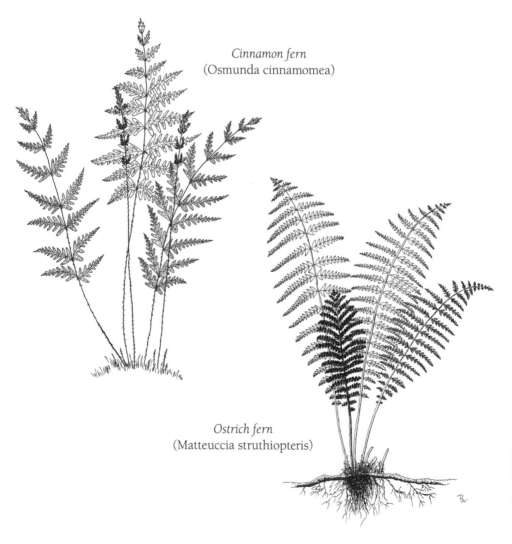

Cinnamon fern
(Osmunda cinnamomea)

Ostrich fern
(Matteuccia struthiopteris)

THE PLAYERS

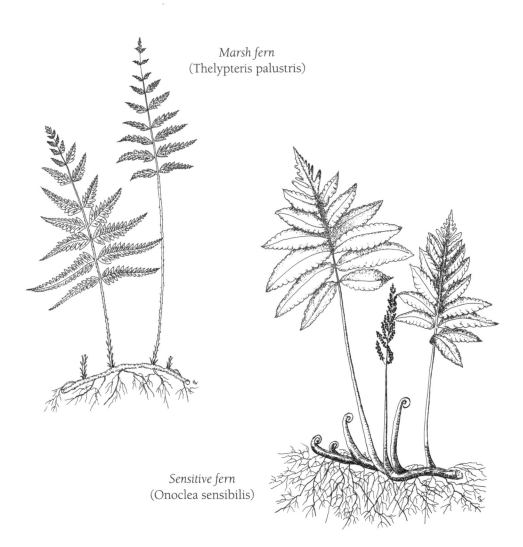

Marsh fern
(Thelypteris palustris)

Sensitive fern
(Onoclea sensibilis)

The marsh fern also has twice-cut fronds. You can distinguish between sterile and fertile fronds by the presence of sori on the fertile fronds, which are also taller and thinner than the sterile fronds.

You need not limit yourself to ponds to discover the fascinating world of ferns. Other ferns grow in habitats such as roadside ditches, meadows, and damp, cool forests, and some even grow out of brick walls.

The sensitive fern is a very common fern with once-cut fronds, found in open fields and swamps. The wavy, lobed fronds do not produce sori, which means that they are sterile. A separate fertile frond appears during the fall. It contains small, brown, bead-shaped clusters containing sori that persist throughout the winter.

The common polypody grows in rock crevices in woodlands. The sori develop on the undersides of the upper lobes. The fronds are once-cut.

The Christmas fern has leathery, evergreen, once-cut fronds with a tough stipe and rachis. The fertile pinnae are limited to the top third of the frond, where there are reddish brown sori on the underside.

The marginal wood fern has large, leathery, evergreen, twice-cut fronds and scaly stipes. The sori are located on the margin of each pinnule. Look for this common fern on rocky woodland slopes.

The bracken fern is common in woodlands and fields. It has very large, leathery, thrice-cut, triangular fronds. Look for sori around the edges of the undersides of pinnules that are folded under.

The lady fern has pointed, thrice-cut fronds with floppy tips. Short, straight, or curved sori develop on the undersides of the fronds. This is a common fern of moist, semishaded woods and fields.

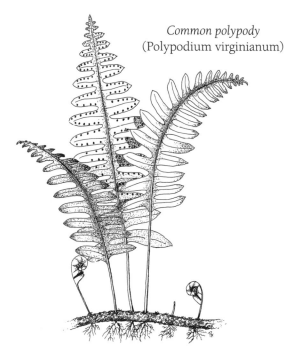

Common polypody
(Polypodium virginianum)

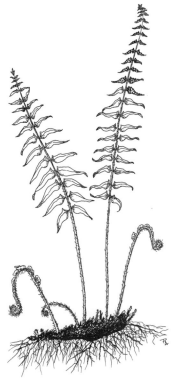

Christmas fern
(Polystichum acrostichoides)

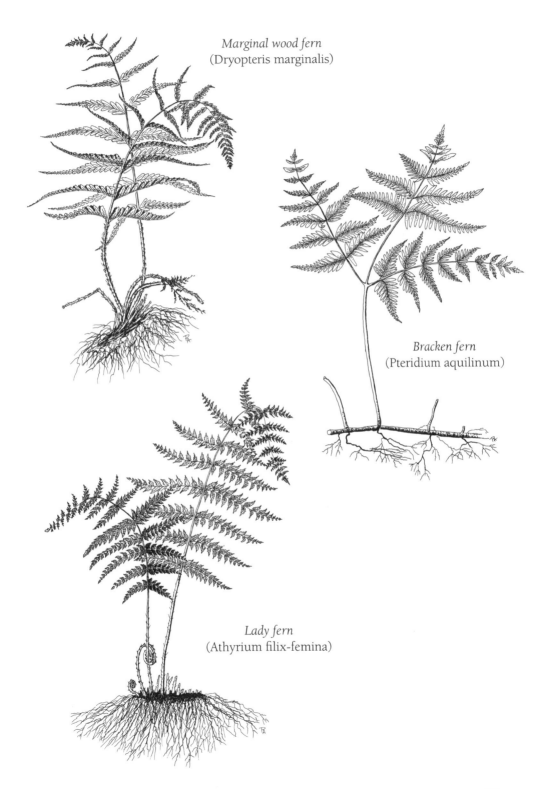

Marginal wood fern
(Dryopteris marginalis)

Bracken fern
(Pteridium aquilinum)

Lady fern
(Athyrium filix-femina)

Fertile versus Sterile Fronds. Although the fronds of most ferns look identical, some of them produce spores and are called fertile fronds; others do not and are known as sterile or vegetative fronds.

Some ferns produce fertile fronds that do not resemble the leafy sterile fronds. The sensitive fern produces fertile fronds that look like small, thin sticks, each with many branchlets. The spore cases look like brown beads decorating the tiny branches. These fertile fronds live long after the sterile fronds have withered and died. The fertile fronds of the cinnamon fern look like cinnamon-colored sticks standing erect in the middle of a clump of bright green sterile fronds.

As you observe your ferns throughout the growing season, look for signs of fertile fronds. When do the fronds first appear? Do they all appear at once? If not, how long is the delay between frond appearance? When do the sori first appear? Are all the look-alike fronds on your fern fertile or are some sterile? When do the fronds, sterile and fertile, die back? On average, what is the lifespan of a frond? How many fronds does one fern produce in a season? Record your findings in your field notebook.

Fiddleheads. In the spring, bright green young ferns begin to poke up through the soil. As each emerges, you will see a coil of green called a fiddlehead, or crosier. These names refers to the coil's shape, the first for its resemblance to the head of a violin, and the second for a bishop's ceremonial staff also called a crosier, which is a stylized shepherd's staff with a crook at the top.

The fiddleheads are coiled because the upper and lower surfaces of the fronds grow at different rates. As the fern grows, the fiddlehead unrolls and expands, revealing tiny new fronds. Sometimes the fiddlehead has a cover of fuzzy, brown scales. Some ferns have a cover of silky hairs on the rachis when the young fiddlehead unrolls. Before the development of synthetic materials, these hairs from large tropical tree ferns were used for upholstery stuffing.

Locate a patch of ferns during the summer months, and return there the following spring to observe the fiddleheads poke through the soil, unfurl, and release their folded leaflets. Record your observations in your field notebook. On what date do you first notice the fiddlehead? Is it wearing a brown, tan, or white fuzzy protective hood? How long does it take to reach its full height? Look for different types of ferns. Do all the ferns you observe have fiddleheads? Which ferns have them and which do not?

In the fall, you can find fiddleheads by poking around the base of the fern. They are tightly coiled, hard, round structures that hug the rhizomes and may be covered by a thin sheet of soil.

Some people relish fiddleheads as tasty vegetables, reminiscent of asparagus. The fiddlehead of commerce is the ostrich fern, great quantities of which are collected in the spring and shipped to markets or canneries. If you would like to investigate this gourmet aspect of ferns, try the following. (*Caution: Do not eat fiddleheads you pick in the wild. Use only those you buy from a grocer.*)

Select fiddleheads that are newly arrived to the grocer's shelves, choosing only those that are bright green and tightly coiled. Cut off the long tails. Between your palms, rub away the fuzzy or brown, papery covering, and wash the fiddleheads well. Steam them until fork-tender, and rinse in cool water. Dry them thoroughly, then toss with a favorite salad dressing. Or if you prefer, stir-fry them in oil with ginger to taste for about two minutes. Add two cloves of garlic, salt, and one-quarter cup of chicken broth. Cover and simmer for about five minutes.

If eating fiddleheads does not appeal to you, you can still buy a few and unfurl them to examine how the leaves are packaged.

Sori and Spores. Summer is the best time to look for ripe spores. You can tell which spores are ripe by the color of the sori, which will be a shiny dark brown. If the sori are white or green, the spores contained within the sporangia are immature. Withered or torn sori indicate that the spores have been dispersed.

On some ferns, the sori are covered with a thin membrane called an indusium, which can be curved, round, or long and narrow. These characteristics of the indusium vary among species and are used to help identify them. The size, shape, color, and location of the sporangia are also important clues in fern identification. The cinnamon fern has clusters of sori on separate stalks. On the ostrich fern, the sori are enveloped by leaflets with curved margins. On the bracken fern, the sori form a continuous line at the frond's edge. The wood fern has scattered rows of sori and a kidney-shaped indusium. The marsh fern has sori near the margins and a kidney-shaped indusium.

When did the spores on your fern mature? Are they on all the green leafy fronds or only on some of them? Where on the frond are they located? Are they confined to the margins of the frond, or are they along the midrib? Are they on a distinctly different fertile frond? Are the sori covered with an indusium? Describe the sporangia. Make a drawing or take a photograph of your fern, perhaps from several different angles. Keep a record of your findings in your field journal.

Remove a mature frond with shiny brown sori and place it between sheets of white paper. In a day or two, remove the top sheet carefully and pick up the frond. Spores should be present on the bottom sheet.

Stipes. With a knife, cut across the stipes of different types of ferns. With the aid of a hand lens, look for the patterns of vascular tubes and compare them on the different ferns. These patterns help identify fern species.

Growth Patterns. Ferns are perennials. After the growing season, the leaves die, but the rhizomes persist. Each spring, new fronds grow from one end of the rhizome, while the other end withers and dies. To see the effect of this growth pattern, you will need to mark off the boundary of a clump of ferns during the growing season. Return to that area in the spring. How has the size and shape of the fern patch changed?

EXPLORATIONS

Propagating Ferns. Unlike trying to grow ferns from spores, this method is relatively simple. You can grow a new plant from almost any part of the fern. Fronds, roots, or rhizomes all will become established and develop into a healthy fern. Two methods for propagating ferns are presented here. For more information about propagating ferns, ask at a local nursery or garden supply shop. There are many methods for propagating ferns.

1. The footed ferns, those that grow with exposed rhizomes, include the common polypody and the fuzzy-footed ferns, which include the bear's foot, rabbit's foot, and squirrel's foot ferns. These names reflect the color of the fuzzy scales that cover the exposed rhizomes. These ferns can be propagated by cutting off pieces of the rhizomes or furry "feet" and securing them in the soil with pieces of bent wire to a depth of about half their thickness.

2. Boston ferns can be propagated from their runners, or stolons, thread-like stems that grow among the fronds and support tiny buds along their length. If you stretch a bud-bearing stolon across some potted soil and clamp it with thin pieces of bent wire, the buds will take root where they touch the soil and produce tiny fernlets. Because the union of gametes (sex cells) is not required in this process, the new fern will be a clone that is identical to the parent fern.

Creating a Terrarium. A terrarium is a tiny greenhouse that will allow you to enjoy ferns throughout the year. To create a terrarium, you will need some simple and easily obtained materials.

Wash a wide-mouthed gallon jar thoroughly with very hot water, then wash it again and allow it to dry. For drainage, line the bottom of the jar with a layer of gravel or small chunks of clay from broken pots to a depth of about one inch. Add about one-quarter inch of charcoal to absorb the gases that decaying vegetation in the soil will produce in the warm, moist environment of the terrarium. At a nursery or supermarket, purchase a small bag of sterile potting soil, and add it to the jar to a depth of about two inches. The soil needs to be light and airy, and potting soil usually contains loam for this purpose.

Ferns best suited for a terrarium are small and slow growing, such as the fragile fern *(Cystopteris fragilis)* and common polypody.

The plants in the terrarium need water, light, heat, and air. How to supply these needs and to what extent they should be supplied will vary according to your particular circumstances. The following suggestions are based on those in *Ferns and Their Allies,* by Edward Frankel.

Light. Put your terrarium near a window where it will receive northern light. Direct rays of the sun will prove deadly. If you prefer, you can use artificial light, which you can control. Place two forty-watt fluorescent tubes about a foot above the terrarium, and light them for about fourteen hours a day. Experiment to find out what conditions are best for your ferns.

Water. The amount of water needed will vary depending on the size of terrarium, where it is located, and the type of ferns planted. You do not want the soil too wet or dry. If the ferns look healthy, you are probably providing the right amount of water.

Air. As the plants need some air, only partially cover the top of the wide-mouthed jar with a small plate of glass or plastic.

How to Learn More. One of the best ways to learn about ferns is to join a group of like-minded people. To find out about groups near your home, write to The American Fern Society, Department of Botany, Milwaukee Public Museum, 800 W. Wells St., Milwaukee, WI 53233-1478, or call the New York Botanical Garden, (718) 817-8700.

CHAPTER 5

Dragonflies and Damselflies

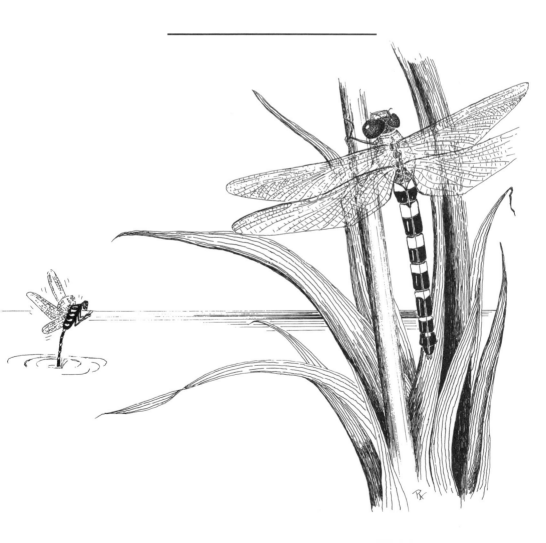

REGAL AERIALISTS

It is one of those sweltering days in July when the air is heavy with wetness. Down at the pond, a few painted turtles, still dripping with green duckweed, climb from the water onto half-sunken logs to sun themselves. Lily pads weighted with insects bob on the surface of the shallow water. The occasional rattle of a lone kingfisher and the *thrump* of a bullfrog break the peaceful silence. But it is the glittering wings and shimmering body of a dragonfly swooping through the heavy summer air that captures the attention.

In the peaceful pond setting that is its favorite habitat, the dragonfly delights the observer. Its shimmering wings are a blur as it hovers almost motionless like a tiny helicopter. In a flash, it darts across the water at high speed and lands deftly on a lily pad. The aerial acrobatics of the dragonfly are matched only by those of the hummingbird and are the envy of aircraft designers.

These aerialists are related to the giant dragonflies that lived in the sultry, swampy forests of the Carboniferous period some 350 million years ago. Fossil evidence indicates that they looked similar to the dragonflies we see today but were considerably larger. Imagine a dragonfly with a wingspan of twenty-eight inches and a long, sleek body swooping in and out of giant ferns at speeds thought to have been in excess of fifty miles per hour. Although dragonflies do not whip through the air at such high speeds today, the wing design responsible for their aerial skills persists.

Dragonflies have two pairs of wings. Each pair can act independently of the other, thus providing the creature with two separate flight surfaces on each side. For the dragonfly, this means increased lift, greater forward propulsion, and reduced drag. Contributing to the dragonflies' strong flight are fan-like reinforcing folds at the base of each wing. The wings are further strengthened and kept rigid by a network of veins.

More recent insects, such as butterflies, have developed a different wing design. In these insects, the two sets of wings are hooked together. This arrangement provides a larger but less flexible flight surface, giving butterflies a slower, more deliberate flight pattern. Butterflies fly slowly but can remain airborne for long periods and can cover long distances. Dragonflies use their speed and maneuverability for catching their airborne insect prey and for escaping their enemies.

Their superb flying ability is only part of their success story. If you try scooping a dragonfly into a butterfly net, you will become aware of another trait that contributes to their success. The difficulty in capturing a dragonfly lies in how they see their world. Two large compound eyes, nearly half the area

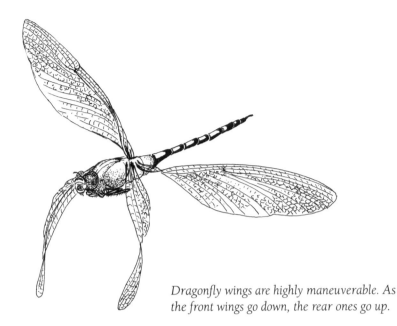

Dragonfly wings are highly maneuverable. As the front wings go down, the rear ones go up.

of the insect's head, extend down the sides of the head. These huge eyes are each made up of ten thousand to thirty thousand tiny windows called facets. Each facet, like an individual eye, is complete with a lens and has its own nerve pathways to the brain. Our eyes, which are designed for detecting very fine detail, each have only one lens but many nerve receptors behind that lens. The dragonfly's eyes, like all insect eyes, are designed primarily to detect the motion of small objects. The mosquito that escapes our notice until it lands and bites is not so lucky when it is in the vicinity of a dragonfly. Some species of dragonflies can detect insect motion as far away as sixty-five feet. Dragonflies also have three more eyes, each marking the corner of a triangle on the top and in front of the insect's head. Additionally, a dragonfly can move its head easily and can cock it at different angles, which probably increases its depth perception.

Dragonflies have two short antennae. Since insects use their antennae as sensory devices, it might seem that dragonflies, with such good vision, would not need these helpers. However, their antennae are used for the senses of touch, hearing, and smell, which provide additional information about conditions in their environment.

While the dragonfly's aerial agility is spectacular, its most notable feature may be the shimmering iridescence of its body and wings flashing in the summer sunlight. The green, blue, bronze, and other metallic hues that make these

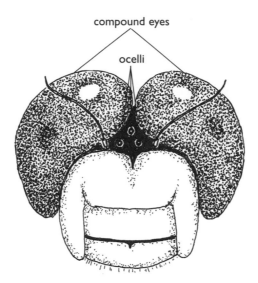

compound eyes

ocelli

In addition to the compound eyes, dragonflies have three simple eyes, called ocelli, which respond to changes in light intensity, triggering changes in insect behavior.

insects so captivating are due to the mechanical scattering of light rays. As light passes through the external covering, or cuticle, that protects the insect's body, tiny structures in that cover cause the light waves to reflect and bend, or refract. Some of the wavelengths are intensified, while others are reduced or eliminated, and it is this mechanical change in the light rays that produces those wonderful iridescent colors. Not all dragonfly colors are mechanically produced, however. The yellows, blacks, and some reds result from pigments embedded in fatty tissue in the exoskeleton. When the insect dies, the fat disintegrates quickly and these colors soon pale, but the colors produced mechanically are slower to fade.

Like all insects, dragonflies cannot produce the heat required for their bodily processes to function efficiently. Their internal temperature or metabolic rate depends on the temperature of the envelope of air that surrounds them, referred to as ambient air. When the temperature of the ambient air is low, the dragonfly's internal temperature is low. As the ambient air warms, the dragonfly's internal temperature rises.

Dragonflies use one of two interesting strategies for regulating body heat: One relies on solar radiation and the other depends on dragonfly metabolism. Dragonflies that rely on the sun to warm them tend to perch a lot. This behavior lets the dragonfly control its body temperature by tilting its body to a near-parallel or near-perpendicular position to the sun's rays. You may have seen a

THE PLAYERS

dragonfly perching with its long, thin abdomen pointed skyward and only the underside facing the sun. In this position, the top of its thorax, or chest, is directed away from the sun, while its wings act as a sunshade. Thus the insect is exposing the smallest possible area to the direct rays of the sun. This is called the obelisk position and is an extreme example of this type of temperature control. Sometimes dragonflies bask on light-colored surfaces and press their wingtips downward. Here, the solar radiation passes through the clear wings and bounces back and forth between the wings and the ground surface, heating the air between. This warms the sides of the thorax where the wing muscles are. Dragonflies that use solar radiation are called heliotherms and come in all sizes. They include most of the typical pond skimmers in the family Libellulidae.

Dragonflies that use their metabolism to regulate their body heat tend not to perch. Instead, they spend the entire day in flight. The heat generated by their wing muscles heats the thorax. There are times when too much heat is produced. When this happens, the dragonfly can pump its body lymph into the usually slender abdomen, which cools the dragonfly. When it is cool, the dragonfly pumps fluid around inside the thorax to speed up heating of the wing muscles. This is often done in the early-morning hours. These dragonflies can control the opening and closing of a valve that separates the thorax from the abdomen. Dragonflies that use this strategy are called endotherms and include the darners (family Aeschnidae).

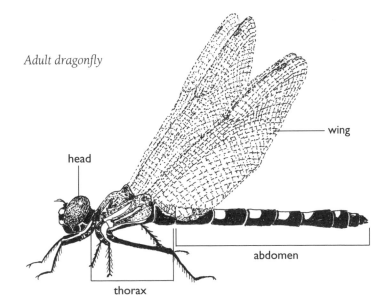

Adult dragonfly

wing

head

abdomen

thorax

Changes in the temperature of ambient air, that envelope of air surrounding the dragonfly, affect its behavior. You can most easily observe these effects early in the morning. After a night sleeping perched on vegetation, the stirring dragonfly is cold. Before it can begin the day's activities, it must warm up its flight muscles. The endotherms do this by wing-whirring, the heliotherms by perching in the sun. In addition, a dragonfly must raise its internal temperature to between 57 and 127 degrees F. before it can begin the challenges of the day, such as hunting, feeding, mating, defending territories, or laying eggs. There is a sense of urgency, because the adult dragonfly has a great deal to do during the next few weeks before its short life is over.

Dragonflies are master hunters that capture their food on the wing. Their long, slender legs, armed with bristles, are held in flight to form a basket used to scoop prey from the air and hold it until the dragonfly can grasp it with its jaws. Their voracious appetite for insects makes these agile predators strong allies in our struggle against adult blackflies and other insects.

If you watch dragonflies long enough, you will eventually see their mating strategies. In one technique, before mating, male dragonflies transfer sperm from the tip of the abdomen to a set of sperm receptacles located under the second abdominal segment. During mating, the male grasps the female by the back of her head with claspers located at the tip of his abdomen, and the female bends her abdomen under and forward to receive the sperm from his receptacles. At this time, they form a sort of circle, and this is called the wheel position. The pair can fly during the wheel position but usually don't, except to fly up to a safe perch away from other males.

If you see dragonflies in tandem, they are not mating, but are engaging in a postmating behavior called contact guarding. The male is protecting his future offspring by flying with the female, stopping here and there to insert the eggs into aquatic plant stems, damp logs, or mudbanks. Such dragonflies are called endophytic egg layers. Almost all damselflies exhibit contact guarding, as do most of the darner dragonflies (family Aeschnidae). Because these males have no territory, the pair flies around the whole pond together.

In non-contact guarding dragonflies, the male and female disconnect after mating and the female lays her eggs directly into the water by tapping her abdomen in flight. This is territorial reproduction. The female is laying eggs in the male's territory while he is hovering nearby, challenging and chasing away other males. The disadvantage to this strategy is that other males can sneak in and steal her. Pond skimmers (family Libellulidae) are largely non-contact guarders, with some exceptions.

Among the pennant dragonflies (see Chapter Note 1) in the Libellulidae family, the male remains attached to the female's head as she taps the water with her abdomen to lay her eggs in open water. Such dragonflies are called exophytic egg layers. Two common dragonflies that use this strategy are the Halloween pennant (*Celithemis eponina*) and the calico pennant (*Celithemis elisa*).

Another variation of contact guarding exists among the saddlebags (*Tramea* sp.). The female breaks away from the male, taps the surface of the water with the tip of her abdomen, releases her eggs, and returns to the clasp of her mate. This performance is done with such rhythm that it appears almost like a dance.

The eggs may take a few days to two weeks to hatch, depending on the temperature of the water—the warmer the water, the more quickly the eggs hatch.

Insect development from egg to adult has some fascinating steps. Some insects, such as butterflies and moths, develop through a four-stage process,

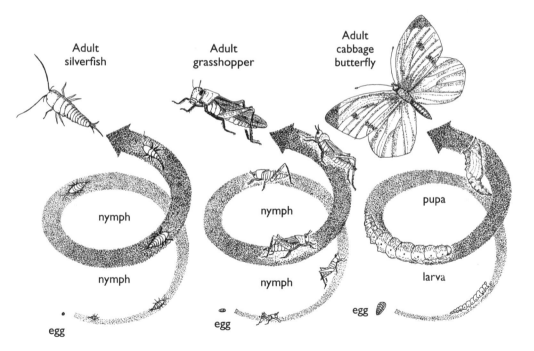

In simple metamorphosis, the only highly visible change is in size.

In incomplete metamorphosis, as the nymph increases in size, it also develops wings and sexual organs.

In complete metamorphosis, the egg hatches into a larva that goes through a pupal stage that develops into an adult completely different in appearance, habitat, and eating habits.

called complete metamorphosis. In each of the stages—egg, larva (caterpillar), pupa, and adult—the insect assumes a completely different appearance. Other insects, such as crickets, develop in a three-stage process, called incomplete, or simple, metamorphosis. The tiny hatchlings look like miniature adults, and the changes that occur during growth and development are less dramatic. As these insects mature, they change in size, but not much in overall appearance.

Dragonflies belong to this latter group, but with an interesting variation. Unlike other insects that undergo incomplete metamorphosis, immature dragonflies, or naiads, are waterbound and do not resemble adults. They undergo a series of molts in which the naiads simply get larger. The naiads are dull green, brown, or other somber color that helps conceal them among pond plants or beneath a film of mud. It is not until the final molt that the familiar dragonfly form appears.

During the immature, or naiad, phase, the dragonfly begins its lifelong occupation as a voracious predator. With an efficient system of jets located in its abdomen, it can propel itself through the water with amazing speed. Powerful jaws at the tip of a long, hinged lower lip, about one-third the length of its body, give this order of insects its official name, Odonata, from the Greek for "tooth." While at rest, this weapon remains folded under the naiad's head.

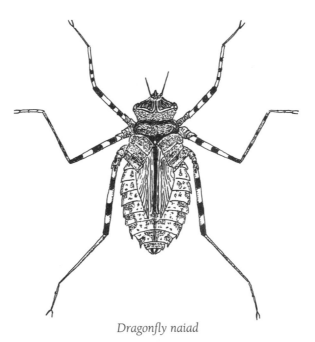

Dragonfly naiad

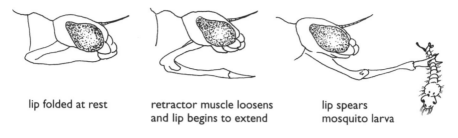

| lip folded at rest | retractor muscle loosens and lip begins to extend | lip spears mosquito larva |

Side view of dragonfly naiad's head showing lower lip

Although the larvae of many insects are devoured by the dragonfly naiads, mosquito larvae are not preferred food. Dragonfly larvae are climbers, sprawlers, and burrowers and they don't often come in contact with mosquito larvae, which thrive just under the surface of the water. Actual studies on dragonfly larval feeding habits show that they feed more heavily on aquatic midges (family Chironomidae), the larvae of moth and sand flies (family Psychodidae), and aquatic earthworms. In a pinch, they will feed on whatever is readily available.

Just before their last molt, soon after dawn or late in the afternoon, naiads climb out of the water and perch on the stems and leaves of plants, logs, rocks, or trees. After breaking out of its tough skin, the newly emerged dragonfly is vulnerable to predators, as its protective external covering dries and slowly begins to harden. Its light-colored, crumpled wings cannot carry it away from danger until they fill with blood. When it eventually flies away, the only evidence that remains of its emergence is the empty skin it left behind.

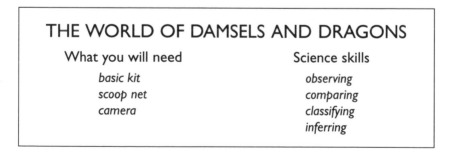

THE WORLD OF DAMSELS AND DRAGONS

What you will need	Science skills
basic kit	*observing*
scoop net	*comparing*
camera	*classifying*
	inferring

OBSERVATIONS

Dragonflies and their close relatives, the damselflies, are two large groups of insects in the order Odonata. In the activities presented here, you will have an opportunity to explore their world. To add to your enjoyment, share these activities with a friend, who can help you make observations.

Dragonflies versus Damselflies. Like all insects, dragonflies and damselflies have six legs (three pairs) and three body parts—head, thorax, and abdomen. As members of the order Odonata, they have two very large compound eyes (dragonflies also have three simple eyes), two short antennae, and a mouth suited for biting and chewing.

On the underside of the thorax are the six legs, and on the top are four membranous wings. The thorax is large compared with the abdomen, because this is where the powerful wing muscles are attached. The wings, which sometimes show iridescent color, always have a network of veins. Scientists use the various patterns of the wing veins to identify dragonfly or damselfly species.

An easy way to distinguish between these two members of the Odonata group is the way they hold their wings when not flying. Dragonflies keep their wings extended horizontally, but damselflies fold their wings over their backs. Damselflies have much thinner bodies than dragonflies, and you can easily observe this difference when the insects are flying. Also, damselflies are weak fliers and stay close to the ground or water or among plants. They can't zip around like dragonflies.

You can get a better look at dragonflies and damselflies if you catch a few and put them in an observation container such as a bug box or other transparent plastic box. You'll also need an aerial or butterfly net, patience, and some knowledge of the takeoff pattern of these insects, discussed below. When you capture these flying machines, make your observations and immediately release them. Remember the naturalist's motto: *Do no harm.*

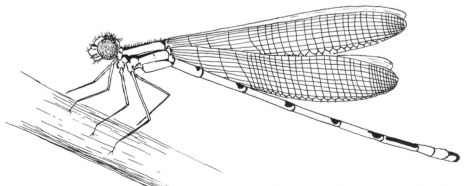

Damselflies are smaller than dragonflies. They have thin bodies and close their wings at rest, whereas dragonflies hold their wings open.

Where to Find Dragonflies and Damselflies. To find these fliers, you need to spend some time at a quiet, weedy pond. Look for a spot where you can sit comfortably for some time and not intrude on the life in and around the pond. If you prefer, you can make your observations while drifting silently in a small boat. Look for their glinting, colorful bodies on a sunny day between eleven in the morning and three in the afternoon. Although they reach their peak numbers in July, you can expect to see them from late spring through the warm days of autumn. Endothermic dragonflies, those that rely on metabolism to regulate body temperature, often fly in the rain. Be on the lookout for the darners (family Aeschnidae) during summer showers.

Sometimes you will hear the whir of their wings as dragonflies or damselflies fly overhead before you actually see them. As you observe them, try to determine whether they are hunting for food, defending territories, looking for mates, or laying eggs.

Dragonflies sometimes appear singly, sometimes in a squadron. How many darting, whirling, hovering dragonflies can you count in one of these clouds? Are there ten, fifteen, twenty, or more?

Dragonfly Flight. Whether dragonflies can fly backward has been a matter of speculation. Some authorities emphatically state that they cannot, while others are not so sure. What do you observe? Do they hover? Do they move ahead or vertically in the air column? Do they flutter their wings while staying in place? Do they actually fly backward, or are they drifting in a breeze? Can you find a dragonfly moving backward without losing altitude? Do you see it fly against the breeze? To determine whether dragonflies do fly backward, you will have to observe more than one dragonfly, and your observations must be carried out on more than one day.

When a storm is approaching, we are often aware of a heaviness in the air. Dragonflies also sense this and fly closer to the ground. On clear, dry days, dragonflies will cruise considerably higher, as do the small insects that nourish them. See if you can observe examples of this behavior on sunny and rainy days.

As you spend some time observing dragonflies, you will notice that some are larger than others. Does there seem to be a relationship between the size of a dragonfly and how high it flies?

Dragonfly Takeoffs. Most people have witnessed a bird takeoff, but they probably don't remember the details of that maneuver. If you can't recall how birds do this, observe it now, using binoculars, and write a description of what the bird does in order to get airborne. You may need to watch more than one bird.

Now observe the takeoff of dragonflies. Do dragonflies seem to start up using similar techniques? In your notebook, describe the differences and similarities between the two takeoff strategies.

It is said that an alarmed dragonfly takes off from a resting place at a forty-five-degree angle. When you find a resting dragonfly, approach it quietly and slowly. When it detects your presence and flies away, note the angle of takeoff. Does it appear to be forty-five degrees? What is the advantage of this information for people studying dragonflies?

Dragonfly and Damselfly Behavior. Spend some time watching a dragonfly or damselfly. It's important that you watch the same insect, or at least the same species, because behavior patterns can vary greatly among species. Observe and record how long the insect remains in flight and how long it perches. Calculate the average time spent in flight and at rest. How do they compare? Keep a record of the maneuvers the insect makes. Does it move horizontally, vertically, backward? Which maneuver is executed most frequently? What landing sites does the insect choose? A males tends to land in the same spot or spots within a small area that it has declared to be its territory. Does it seem to prefer landing on particular types of vegetation? Is each landing site the same distance aboveground?

Dragonflies and Damselflies Close-up. Spend some time observing dragonflies and damselflies at rest. Record your observations. Look at the wings. Can you see a network of veins? Are the wings stiff or floppy? Are they colored? What is the shape of the insect's body? Does it taper toward the tip? What color or colors is the body? Are there any markings on the face or head? Are the damselfly bodies as brightly colored as those of the dragonflies? How does the head differ from that of a dragonfly? Do they have compound eyes? How many different colored dragonflies and damselflies can you find? In addition to making notes, you may wish to draw or photograph the insects you observe.

Dragonfly Identification. Although several species of dragonflies prefer stream habitats, those listed here are most likely to be seen around ponds.

Common Skimmers (Family Libellulidae). Most of the dragonflies you find will be members of this large group. These insects have brightly colored bodies that, at one to one and a half inches (a few are larger), are shorter than their wingspan. Their wings have colored bands or spots. Males and females are often colored differently. They are fast, erratic fliers that often hover.

Darners (Family Aeschnidae). These dragonflies generally range in size from two and one-fourth to three and one-half inches. The green darner (*Anax junius*) is a common pond dweller. The metallic green thorax and bluish abdomen are easy to spot even when the insect is on the wing. A close look will reveal a targetlike mark on the head.

Green-eyed Skimmers (Family Corduliidae). These dragonflies are usually black and may have a metallic shimmer but seldom have light markings. Wings are clear, with an occasional small, dark spot at the base. Bodies are about one and one-half to two and three-fourths inches long. Look for the bright green eyes. These skimmers fly in straight lines, which may be interrupted by periods of hovering.

Belted Skimmers (Family Macromiidae). These dragonflies are light brown with light markings on the chest, or thorax. They are about two and one-fourth to two and three-fourths inches long. Look for these uncommon dragonflies along the boggy shores of ponds.

Damselfly Types. Damselfly species can be difficult to identify. The descriptions provided here will help you determine the family.

Spread-winged Damselflies (Family Lestidae). These damselflies are most easily identified by the partial spread of the wings over the body when at rest. The clear wings are reinforced at the base for added strength. Bodies vary in length from one and one-fourth to two inches. Look for these damselflies at the edges of ponds or freshwater marshes, where they rest on plant or grass stems.

Narrow-winged Damselflies (Family Coenagrionidae). This large family contains more species of damselflies than any other. They are weak fliers, and when resting, they hold the body horizontally, with the wings held at right angles to the body. The males are generally more colorful than the females. Bluets (*Enallagma* sp.) are the largest group and have clear wings. Most have blue bodies with black markings, but a few are red or yellow. Another species, the violet dancer (*Argia violacea),* is identified by the violet color of the males. Blackish damselflies with red abdomens belong to the genus *Amphiagrion.* Most species have colorless wings, but the wings of *Argia fumipennis* are smoky brown in some parts of its range, although they are clear in the Northeast.

Broad-winged Damselflies (Family Calopterygidae). These large damselflies, with bright, metallic bodies, are generally seen close to woodland streams. The males of the most common broad-winged damselflies display black wings and a greenish body.

Egg Laying. Some species deposit their eggs by dipping their abdomens into the water as they fly; others insert their eggs into plant stems, damp logs, and mudbanks. Virtually all damselflies are endophytic egg layers, laying their eggs in plant stems. They will sometimes submerge for up to half an

The male dragonfly sometimes remains attached to the mated female while she releases her eggs into the water.

hour, climbing backward down an aquatic plant stem all the way to the pond bottom, laying eggs in the stem as they go. Some species lay their eggs in emergent plants well above water level, the eggs not contacting the water until the following fall when the plant dies. Look for the females clinging to reeds or other plants, with their abdomens thrust below the surface of the water. They are probably depositing their eggs. You also may see dragonflies or damselflies flying in tandem.

Naiads. Odonata naiads spend their life in the water and can be loosely grouped as climbers, sprawlers, or burrowers. Climbers move slowly among dense pond vegetation in quiet waters and include the narrow-winged damselflies (family Coenagrionidae).

Sprawlers have long legs, are slow moving, and come in drab colors. These bottom dwellers include the common skimmer dragonflies (family Libellulidae). The green-eyed skimmers (family Corduliidae) also have sprawling naiads that lie on the pond's sandy bottom, where they dig out the sand or silt beneath them and sink into the hole.

Burrowers are primarily naiads that live in streams and rivers. Burrowing is an adaptation for living in flowing water and helps keep the naiads from being washed downstream by strong currents. Spiketails (family Cordulegastridae) have burrowing larvae, but none of them are pond dwellers. Clubtails (family Gomphidae), which also have burrowing naiads, are primarily river and stream dwellers, but there are several species that do burrow in pond muck, including the unicorn clubtail (*Arigomphus villosipes*).

To find Odonata naiads, you will have to scoop up some pond muck with a dip net or kitchen strainer. Pour the contents of the net, along with some pond water, into a collecting container. With some luck, you will have captured a naiad or two.

What color are the naiads? Can you find the great, prey-grabbing lower lip? Are there featherlike gills at the end of the body? How many? Does the naiad use these gills for swimming? If there are no gills to be seen, how does it move? Can you identify any of the creatures as a dragonfly or damselfly naiad? Use the accompanying illustrations to help you. Write any additional questions you may have about these insects in your field notebook. You may learn the answers as you continue your observations.

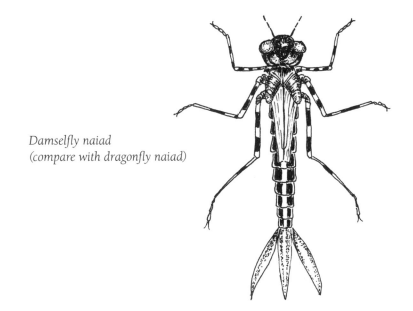

Damselfly naiad
(compare with dragonfly naiad)

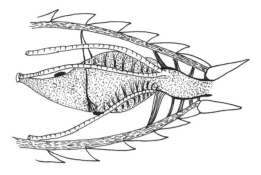

Dragonfly naiads have rectal gills; damselfly naiads possess caudal gills at the end of the tail.

Dragonfly naiads have a respiratory trick not found in other waterbound insects. They have ten abdominal segments, and abdominal gills are located at about the fourth and fifth segments. Water is drawn into the abdominal cavity through an opening at the tip of the abdomen. The water aerates the gills inside the abdomen and is then squirted out through the tip with enough force to propel the naiad forward. The burrowing naiad of some clubtails has an elongated snorkel-like tip on its abdomen so that it can obtain clear water for its gills while remaining burrowed in the substrate.

Damselfly naiads obtain oxygen from the water in a different way. At the end of their abdomens are long, thin appendages with gills that vary in size and color among species. The gills contain air tubes that divide many times to produce a network of tubules. The tubules carry oxygen to all parts of the naiad's body and excrete carbon dioxide to the water. The gills are as fragile as they look and are easily broken off, but they will grow back. The gills work in conjunction with the body surface as organs of respiration.

Pond Food Chains. Dragonflies and damselflies feed on many different small animals, and they provide food for a wide range of other creatures. The larvae are nourished by small fish, insect larvae, tadpoles, pond snails, and worms and in turn are important food sources for waterbirds, big fish, frogs, salamanders, water beetles, and spiders. Adult Odonata eat moths, wasps, flies, beetles, and bees and provide food for fish, frogs, insect-eating plants such as sundews, and a variety of birds.

How many food chains can you discover at your pond? Make a diagram that shows those different food chains. Food chains interlace to form complex food webs. Make a simple food web from the food chains you observe.

Here are samples of some food chains that you might see:

In the water:

1. mosquito larvae > dragonfly and damselfly larvae > water beetles
2. very small fish > dragonfly and damselfly larvae > frogs
3. freshwater worms > dragonfly and damselfly larvae > wading birds
4. dragonfly and damselfly larvae > pike and trout > humans
5. dragonfly and damselfly larvae > water spiders > birds

On land:

1. blackflies > dragonfly and damselfly adults > spiders
2. beetles > dragonfly and damselfly adults > carnivorous plants
3. bees > dragonfly and damselfly adults > birds > cats
4. dragonfly and damselfly adults > birds > cats

Dragonflies and damselflies need more than a pond and some food to survive; they require a habitat that will nurture them throughout their entire life cycle. Larvae need fallen logs, weedy stems, and other objects that jut out of the water to climb onto when they are ready for their final molt. Adult Odonata need perching places as well. They are territorial and need space. But sadly, trees, shrubs, and plants at the water's edge are disappearing, and ponds are drying up. Dragonflies and damselflies also are under increasing stress from pesticides and other chemicals used in farming and manufacturing.

We can do a great deal to help these fascinating fliers in their struggle for survival. If we create ponds in municipal parks and on our properties when space and zoning regulations permit, the Odonata will come. They need little encouragement to make their home in a new habitat. What a tragedy it would be to lose these beautiful insects because of indifference.

CHAPTER NOTE

1. Skimmers are now called pennants. The common name for these dragonflies was standardized in the last few years by the Dragonfly Society of America. The new name refers to their perching behavior in naked stems of grasses or other vegetations where they look like little pennants. The new names do not yet appear in many field guides.

CHAPTER 6

Butterflies

WINGED FLOWERS

On a serene summer morning, sitting along the margin of a stream, I watched delicate winged air dancers flutter among the jewelweed and loosestrife. They danced in silence as the water gurgled over rock and log on its long journey to the sea. At moments like this, one can easily agree with Robert Frost that butterflies indeed "are flowers that fly and all but sing."

On their forays through wet places in search of energy-giving nectar, butterflies have provided memorable experiences for many of us. Yet what are these kaleidoscopes of color that have joined wildflowers and birds as outdoor pleasures?

For most of their life cycle, butterflies bear no resemblance to the beautiful adults that spawned them. These remarkable insects experience complete metamorphosis (from the Greek for "change"). Butterflies begin their lives as eggs laid singly or in clusters on the vegetation of plants that will be food for the hatchlings. Each of the nearly fifteen thousand species of butterflies found worldwide produces eggs that are unique in size, color, and texture, posing great identification problems for taxonomists (the scientists who identify and categorize living things).

When it leaves the egg, the butterfly is a tiny caterpillar called a larva, with a voracious appetite and mouthparts made for chewing and chomping. It is a virtual eating machine whose sole purpose is storing fat and protein, which must nourish not only the larva but also the emergent butterfly it will become. In its next stage as a pupa, it will not eat at all, and as an adult butterfly, it will sip nectar for energy to sustain life functions and flight rather than for growth.

Like lobsters, grasshoppers, and other arthropods, the caterpillar must shed its tough external skin from time to time to accommodate its growing body. A caterpillar molts several times before entering the pupal phase.

Before becoming a pupa, a caterpillar seeks out a place where it can attach and become a chrysalis, usually on a plant or leaf stem, or sometimes on some other stable surface. Each species of caterpillar begins to pupate in a slightly different way. About twenty-four hours after securing itself to the plant of choice with silken threads, the caterpillar molts for the last time. When the old skin drops off, a soft and tender-skinned pupa emerges. In this unprotected state, the pupa is susceptible to attack from predators such as spiders and an array of parasites. When the new skin hardens, it forms a tough outer casing like a small fort. At this point the pupa is called a chrysalis. The chrysalis presents new defenses against would-be assailants, although long periods of drought or excessive moisture can present dangers to the chrysalis as well.

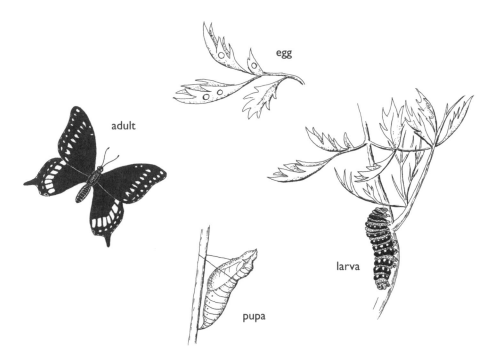

Life cycle of a swallowtail butterfly

The pupal, or chrysalid, phase in the butterfly life cycle may appear to be a period of rest, but in fact, it is a time of incredible change. If we could look inside the chrysalis, what we would see would bear no resemblance to the architect that built it. Responding to chemical signals, larval structures break down into a cellular stew. Out of this melange of fat, protein, and rudimentary materials, a helpless butterfly with crumpled wings will emerge. In a relatively short time, those wings will become functional and the butterfly will flutter away.

The length of time that butterflies pupate varies with the species and with the season. The mourning cloak butterfly, which overwinters as an adult, pupates for about two or three weeks in the summer, whereas hairstreaks, overwintering as pupae, may remain in this state for six months or more. Some swallowtail butterflies also overwinter as pupae. The size, color, and structure of the chrysalis are also unique to each species. Some are green, others are brown, and some species have both green and brown chrysalises. Some are beautifully decorated, and others are quite plain. If you want to find the chrysalis of a particular butterfly, it is helpful to know the food plants of the caterpillar. Knowing this is not a foolproof method for finding a chrysalis, however, because pupation is not always on a food plant. Winter, when most plants have no leaves, is a good time to look for chrysalises.

Through its complex life cycle, each species of butterfly occupies two distinctly different ecological niches: one niche as a caterpillar, with its special food requirements, and the other as an adult, needing different sources of food. This strategy has worked well, as modern butterflies have been around for about 26 million years, and fossil evidence shows that their ancestral forms date as far back as 100 million years.

Butterflies' wings are covered with scales. Although you can't see individual scales without the aid of a powerful magnifier, they come in a variety of sizes and shapes. Some are square, some are round, and some are long and narrow. If you have ever handled a butterfly, you have probably noticed the slippery, sparkling dust that remains on your fingertips after the butterfly gets away. This talclike material is made up of microscopic scales that easily slide off the wings, a quality that facilitates the butterfly's escape from tight places such as a spiderweb or a predator's grasp. Shedding a few scales is of little consequence to the butterfly, but if the supporting veins in the wing membrane become crushed or broken in a struggle for freedom, the butterfly can become unbalanced and unable to fly well, making an easy meal for birds and other predators.

Each scale is so small that it takes tens of thousands of them to cover one-half of a square inch. If you were to look at a scale under a high-powered microscope, you would see a hollow structure much like the frame of a house, with struts, posts, and a great deal of space. Incorporated into the structure are pigment granules, so if a butterfly lost all its scales, it would be colorless. Many butterflies' soft earth tones are due to melanin, pteridines, and other color-producing chemicals that are by-products of metabolic activity during the pupal phase. Other colors are caused by the manipulation of light as it is reflected, refracted, and scattered through the architecture of individual scale cells. Specific color patterns in the wings are unique to each butterfly species. Scientists once thought that the scales' purpose was to provide structural reinforcement, but a newer theory suggests that they help prevent heat loss during the cooler nights.

Generally, you will not see butterflies fluttering through the air until eight or nine in the morning. In order to mate or lay eggs, butterflies must fly, and they cannot do so unless their internal temperature is around 82 to 100 degrees F. (28 to 38 degrees C.). Unlike mammals, butterflies cannot control their body temperature through internal mechanisms. Their internal temperature is regulated by the temperature of the ambient air, the envelope of air that surrounds them. After cooling down during the night, butterflies have developed a neat trick called basking, which helps them absorb the heat of the early-morning sun. The basic scientific principle controlling this process is very simple: Dark colors absorb light and heat, and light colors reflect light and heat. Thus different butterflies must use different strategies to obtain heat from sunlight.

Some butterflies have dark inner wing areas on the upper wing surfaces near their dark bodies. These butterflies bask in direct sunshine with the wings held flat, outstretched horizontally on each side of the body. In this position, the heat from the sun is absorbed by the dark wing area. Heat flows from this dark wing area to the body and also from the dark abdomen and thorax into the body muscles. Heat absorbed by the outer sections of the wing is not useful because it is lost to the cool air. You may see swallowtail butterflies in this position.

Other butterflies use the lower surfaces of their wings to absorb the sunlight. These butterflies bask holding both wings together and straight up over the body. For these butterflies, it does not matter what color the upper wing surface might be, but the undersides of the wings must be dark colors.

The third method of basking is really very clever. These butterflies bask by holding their wings in a V over the body. They need a light-colored upper wing surface to reflect light down the V to the dark body, which absorbs the reflected light. If they use a wide V, only the wing area near the body reflects sunlight to the body, and this section of the wing must be white or light in color. If they use a narrow V, the whole wing surface reflects light down to the body, and the whole upper wing surface must be light in color.

Tiny cabbage butterfly holds its wings together to bask, while swallowtail butterfy extends its wings to the side while basking.

During the day, when the ambient temperature increases, some butterflies will have to cool down. They can accomplish this by resting with the body in the shade of the wings. Another technique is to fly or perch at higher elevations. Butterflies are most efficient when the ambient temperature is 60 to 108 degrees F. (16 to 42 degrees C.).

Flying is expensive in terms of energy, and to meet the cost of the activity, butterflies must have a supply of energy-rich food. The caterpillar's mouthparts have developed into a flexible, strawlike proboscis that does the job efficiently. This long, narrow tube is coiled when the butterfly is not drinking nectar. When the butterfly feeds, it extends the proboscis into the flower's nectar chamber, and muscles inside the butterfly's head create a partial vacuum so that external air pressure forces the sugary nectar up into its mouth. It is similar to when we suck a drink through a straw. The length and diameter of the proboscis are related to the energy the butterfly must expend to draw up the nectar. The amount of suction required is related to the sugar content and the resulting thickness of the liquid. The higher the sugar content, the thicker the nectar, and the more energy the butterfly must expend to drink it. This process is called siphoning-sucking and is not used by those insects with

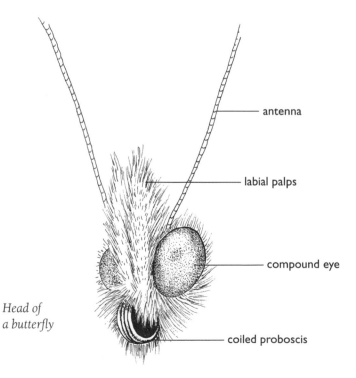

antenna

labial palps

compound eye

*Head of
a butterfly*

coiled proboscis

mouthparts designed for piercing or chewing. It is not known whether butterflies can regulate their suction pressure so that they can drink nectar regardless of how viscous it is or whether they can change the diameter and length of the suction tube. These are questions that scientists are presently exploring.

Butterflies are so beautiful that it's difficult to think of them as nourishment for other living things, but they are preyed upon by birds, reptiles, and other creatures. To avoid becoming a meal, butterflies have developed some clever strategies to conceal their presence. The vast number of intricate scales plays an important role in this deception. Even though they are expensive to produce and maintain in terms of the energy, the protection they offer outweighs their cost.

One very effective use of the scales is called cryptic coloration, or camouflage. In this strategy, the butterfly blends into its background. Sometimes the upper surface of the wings is brightly colored, while the undersurface consists of muted browns and tans. These and other earth tones help the butterfly blend in with tree bark, rock, patches of dirt, and other places where it rests with its wings folded up, hiding the bright colors.

Butterflies use various kinds of mimicry to avoid predators. Some butterflies disguise themselves through the use of flash patterns. These patterns include eyespots on the wings, which when exposed, look like large eyes and frighten would-be predators. Buckeyes and wood nymphs use this defense mechanism. Eyespots vary among species in size, position, number, and color. The viceroy butterfly mimics the coloration of the foul-tasting, toxic monarch. This form of deception helps viceroys avoid hungry predators. Hairstreaks, swallowtails, and tailed blues have tailed hind wings that resemble antennae and accompanying spots that mimic eyes. (The loss of a hind-wing tail to a predator does not significantly impair flight ability.) The deception continues through the subdued color of the head and the curious behavior of walking backward on a leaf or twig.

Butterflies have large, compound eyes made up of thousands of individual lenses. Their vision is good, although they are quite nearsighted. They have good color vision, and the compound eye provides a keen ability to detect nearby motion that might signal an approaching predator. They see the same colors as we see, as well as ultraviolet and infrared wavelengths.

Like many other living things, butterflies are telling us something about the state of the environment. For some time, biologists have been studying one of the checkerspots that makes its home on the West Coast. This butterfly is helping scientists explore the impact that a warming trend is having on their preferred habitat. Over the past hundred years, these butterflies have been moving into higher latitudes and elevations, where it is cooler. The butterflies still live in western North America but are leaving their southernmost limit in Mexico and gaining a foothold in Canada.

The conversion of wild places for human purposes, such as for agriculture, forestry, commercial and residential use, as well as overzealous application of insecticides and herbicides have been reflected by a decline in butterfly populations. Are we listening?

THE WORLD OF BUTTERFLIES

What you will need	Science skills
basic kit	*observing*
binoculars	*comparing*
camera	*identifying*

OBSERVATIONS

Butterfly watching has replaced butterfly collecting, and gardeners plant flowers that provide food for caterpillars and butterflies. Pins and mounting boards have yielded to binoculars and cameras, as live specimens delight observers more than preserved ones. You can begin your adventures with butterflies by doing the activities presented here.

When and Where to Look. In the warmer parts of the country, you can observe butterflies throughout most of the year. In cooler regions, you can expect to see butterflies from April to the first few fall frosts. The farther north you travel, the more the beginning of the butterfly season will be delayed.

Unlike birds, which often sing before the sun is above the horizon, butterflies don't stir unless the air is sufficiently warm, usually between about 9 A.M. and 6 P.M., depending on the time of year. Butterflies are found wherever their larval food plants and adult nectar plants are located. Once you find a food source preferred by adult butterflies, all you have to do is wait and watch. A botanical garden or a local park with floral gardens is a good place to begin your adventure.

Butterflies versus Moths. Butterflies often remain in one place for an extended period of time, frequently long enough for you to get a good look at them. Butterflies and moths share many similar characteristics, which frequently makes it difficult to tell them apart. The fact that some moths are daytime fliers only adds to the confusion. The accompanying chart will help you distinguish butterflies from moths.

	Butterfly	Moth
antennae	slender with club at tip	hairlike or feathery
body	smooth and slender	fuzzy or hairy and stout
wings	large relative to body weight; rounded; held vertically at rest for many species	elongated; when at rest, lie flat like shingles on a roof; hook-and-bristle coupling keeps forewing and hind wing together in flight
flight	smooth and graceful; a series of flaps followed by a glide for many species, but not all	stiff and erratic; a series of uninterrupted flaps; no gliding

Mourning cloak butterfly
(Nymphalis antiopa)

Virgin tiger moth
(Gramonia virgo)

Butterflies and moths have so many similar traits that it is often difficult to distinguish them from each other.

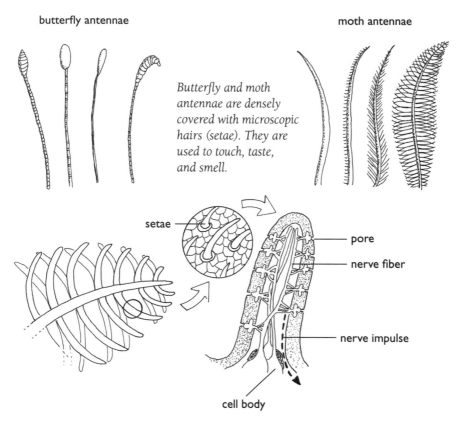

butterfly antennae

moth antennae

Butterfly and moth antennae are densely covered with microscopic hairs (setae). They are used to touch, taste, and smell.

setae

pore

nerve fiber

nerve impulse

cell body

This enlarged view of seta shows how messages are passed to the central nervous system.

The most reliable of these characteristics are the antennae, or feelers. If the antennae have a swelling, or club, at their tip, you have found a butterfly. Butterflies and moths both use their antennae for the sense of smell. Millions of odor-sensitive cells in the antennae guide the butterfly to flowers. The antennae also act as balance and orientation organs.

Wings. Butterfly wings have practical functions. They are for flying, courting, avoiding predators, and regulating body temperature. Each butterfly has a pair of hind wings and a pair of forewings. If you look closely at these wings while a butterfly is perching, you will see cells or spaces bordered by a network of veins. Scientists use the size and shape of these spaces to identify various species of butterflies.

Most butterflies rest with the wings folded back or up (vertically) over the body. In this position, you can see that many of the common butterflies have more subdued, less flashy colors on the undersides of the wings. This provides camouflage so the butterfly can hide from predators. The mourning cloak butterfly shows a broad yellow band along the edge of the upper surface of the wing when flying. When resting on a tree trunk, the butterfly is well camouflaged by the barklike pattern and colors of the underwing. No yellow is visible.

Look for butterflies on flowers, tree trunks, or any other places they might land where you can easily observe them. Are the colors and patterns on the upper and lower surfaces of the wings the same or different? Do the wings have bands, spots, or other designs? Where are these located? Are the wing edges wavy or straight? Do the hind wings have pointed tails?

Flight Patterns. Observe a butterfly in flight and describe the pattern. Is it rapid or slow? Does it fly high or close to the grass? Does it fly in a straight line? Is the flight smooth or jerky? Would you describe it as a flap and glide kind of flying? (Monarchs, swallowtails, and many of the brushfoots do this.)

Butterfly Behavior. Butterflies have their own distinctive habits and behavior patterns. On a hot, sunny day, you will see American coppers dart at every passing object, including you. Compare that behavior with that of the easygoing satyrs, purposeful fritillaries, sedate monarchs, and vacillating blues. Some always seem hungry and in a hurry to fly from one blossom to another, while others spend long periods sunning themselves. Describe the behavior of the butterflies you find.

The vivid orange and dark brown upper wings of the American copper are quite distinctive. At rest, however, the American copper appears a dull yellow.

Basking. Butterflies often bask when they need to warm up their flight muscles. Do you find any examples of this behavior? Examine the photographs of upper and lower surfaces of wings of living specimens in various field guides, and try to predict how some of the butterflies bask. Do you think they bask with wings in shallow or deep Vs, or with their wings folded vertically?

Feeding. When a butterfly lands on a flower, spend some time watching, and you may see it uncoil its proboscis and feed. Can you see where it inserts the proboscis? How long does it spend at each flower?

Puddling. Butterflies need salts and materials rich in nitrogen in their diet, in addition to the energy-rich sugar. Since butterflies eat only plant nectar and sometimes sap and rotting fruit juice, all of which lack salt, they must find salts in other sources. These winged creatures obtain these nutrients from the water in puddles that form on dirt roads and on paths along the margins of streams, ponds, and other wet places. You may see groups of butterflies gathered where there is little or no water present. As evaporation proceeds, the concentration of salts increases, and the butterflies gather up the nutrients that remain on the dry earth by moistening the soil with saliva. This dissolves the nutrients, which they then draw up through their proboscises. Carrion of foxes and other animals, as well as dung, also supply needed salts and amino acids.

The puddling populations are made up of males, which pass along the salts to females when mating. The salt aids in protecting the eggs and also may enhance male pheromones, chemicals that attract females.

Look for butterflies engaged in puddling. Blues, tiger swallowtails, hackberries, and sulphurs are frequent visitors to roadside puddles. Sulphurs sometimes gather by the hundreds. You also may see great spangled fritillaries, anglewings, satyrs, cabbage whites, American coppers, and buckeyes. You can try to attract butterflies to a puddle by placing a small square of white paper close to the rim.

Butterfly Identification. Many people find joy simply in watching butterflies, but others like to know the names of the butterflies they see. For those who like to categorize living things, the following is an introduction to butterflies you might find in wet places. Included are several families of butterflies and skippers found east of the Mississippi. Generally these families can be distinguished by such characteristics as the shape, size, and color of their wings, as well as flight behaviors.

Mothlike Butterflies

Skippers (family Hesperiidae). These butterflies are quite mothlike in appearance. They have thicker bodies than other butterflies and relatively wide heads. Their antennae have the butterfly's requisite club, but each is tipped

Silver-spotted skipper
(Epargyreus clarus)

with a hook. Members of the group have a characteristic swift, darting, erratic flight as they skip from flower to flower, and that, along with the dark brown coloration of many of the species, may make it difficult to identify these butterflies, but don't be discouraged. Without much experience, you can identify skippers at a distance by their characteristic resting positions. Some skippers hold their wings in the fold-wing position, with the forewings in a V and the hind wings horizontal to the body. Another group, known as the spread-winged skippers, hold the wings flat in a more typical butterfly position.

The upper surfaces of many skipper wings are generally dull orange to brown with light spots, while the underwings are typically darker, with faint spots. A few of the smaller skippers have a greenish tinge on the underside. Few have distinct white or silver spots on the underside.

True Butterflies

Swallowtails (family Papilionidae). These butterflies are probably the most commonly known. They are colorful and large and are best known for the long tails that project from their hind wings. Their wingspan extends about two to six inches. Their slow, drifting flight makes them easy to observe. There are many different types of swallowtail butterflies. Those found in wet places are generally black, yellow, and deep blue, with red, yellow, and whitish markings. The common tiger swallowtail is found in moist, wooded areas. They are frequent visitors at puddles, where they drink water for its salt content. Swallowtail flight is strong and intermittent gliding.

Whites and Sulphurs (family Pieridae). These familiar butterflies have white, yellow, or orange wings with simple black marking or none at all. They are small to medium butterflies, with wingspans of one and three-fourths to

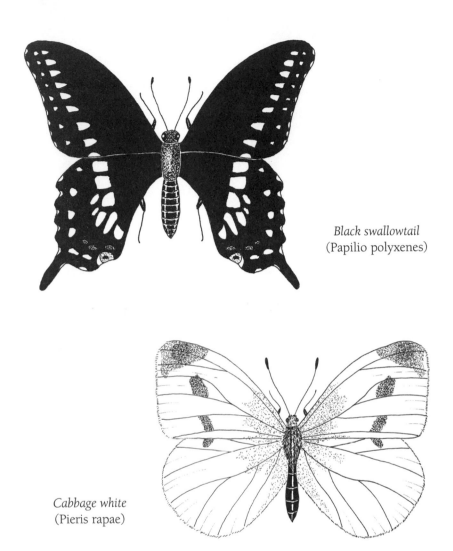

Black swallowtail
(Papilio polyxenes)

Cabbage white
(Pieris rapae)

two and three-fourths inches, although some are larger. The cabbage whites are among the best known, as they feed on food crops. Although conspicuous, these butterflies are not desirable to predators, as they taste bad due to mustard oils obtained from their host plants during the larval stage. Most whites and sulphurs breed many times, so you can expect to see them throughout the butterfly season. Look for them gathered at puddles.

Gossamer wings (family Lycaenidae). These butterflies are usually small, one to two inches, and their names reflect their colors or structures. The blues are usually iridescent. Most hairstreaks have a tiny, hairlike tail on the hind wings. The coppers are frequently copper colored.

Metalmarks (family Riodinidae). Most metalmarks do not frequent wet places. They usually perch with wings open flat or cocked slightly. The wings of the metalmarks are dotted with silver metallic spots.

Brushfooted butterflies (family Nymphalidae). This is a very large family of butterflies. The name brushfoot refers to the front legs, which are reduced in length, lack claws, and are not used for walking. This is a helpful identification mark, because they seem to have only four legs instead of the usual six. As a group, they are strong, rapid fliers, a characteristic that makes them difficult to identify while on the wing. Only those subfamilies with members that visit wet places are listed here with some of their identifying features.

Milkweed butterflies (subfamily Danaidae). These butterflies are named for the larval food plant, milkweed, which produces a milky sap. Toxins contained in the sap are ingested by the caterpillar and are incorporated into the tissues of the adult. The toxins make the insect taste bad and induce vomiting, thus preventing them from being eaten by birds.

The most well-known milkweed butterflies are the monarch and queen butterflies. They are fairly large, with a wingspan of three and three-fourths to four and seven-eighths inches. Small swellings on the black veins of the hind wings, which are actually pheromone scent patches, identify the males. Monarchs are probably most well known for migrating thousands of miles to special places in the mountainous fir forests of central Mexico. They are large, brilliantly colored, and attract attention wherever they fly.

Look for these butterflies wherever milkweed is found between June and October in the South and August and September in the cooler northern United

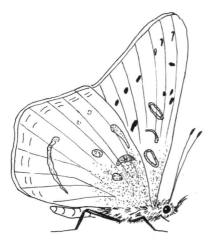

A brushfoot
Note the greatly reduced front leg.

Monarch butterfly
(Danaus plexippus)

Queen
(Danaus gilippus)

States and Canada. Their bold orange color is marked with black and punctuated with white spots.

Satyrs (subfamily Satyridae). These medium-size gray or brown butterflies have brightly colored eyespots on the undersides of their wings. Some members of the family are common and widespread. They can be identified by their characteristically jerky and fluttering flight pattern as they weave through vegetation close to the ground, where their drab colors keep them well hidden from predators. They lay their eggs in the grass, which becomes food for the emerging larvae. Satyrs rely on behavioral strategies and camouflage to protect them from predators. Temperature affects their behavior. At 60 degrees F. they will perch, but as the temperature climbs above 75, they will spend most of their time flying. The northern pearly-eye spends time in

Pearly eye
(Enoida *sp.*)

damp, deciduous woods, while the Appalachian brown flies in wet, wooded swamps, marshes, and wet meadows, where it erratically weaves through sedges and grasses. Look for these butterflies between June and September. Satyrs puddle and are drawn to carrion, urine, and tree sap. They are also found in moist, wet vegetation.

Fritillaries (subfamily Nymphalinae). The meadow fritillary has a wingspan of one and five-eighths to two inches. The orange and black pattern on the upper surface of the forewings resembles a checkerboard. Look for these butterflies in tall, weedy, wet meadows and marshes, where violets are a larval food.

Viceroys and white admirals (subfamily Limenitidinae). The viceroy butterfly can be identified by its flap and glide pattern of flight and its orange and black coloration. With a wingspan of two and five-eighths to three and five-sixteenths inches, it is smaller than the similar monarch butterfly. The name carries some humor with it: Because it looks like a monarch but is smaller, it only gets the rank of a viceroy, or the king's assistant.

Baltimore checkerspots and mourning cloaks (subfamily Nymphalinae). These butterflies are orange, black, and brown. The Baltimore checkerspot has several rows of white dots on the outer half of both pairs of wings. Turtlehead, a member of the snapdragon family found in woodlands, along streambanks, and elsewhere in wet grounds, is a favorite food.

The mourning cloak butterfly has wings with wavy outer edges and a bold yellow band on both pairs of wings. With a lifespan of about eleven months, these butterflies probably live longer than any other species.

BUTTERFLIES OF WET PLACES
AND THE PLANTS THAT FEED THEM

Butterfly	Food Source	Location
Swallowtail Family		
pipevine swallowtail	adult nectar—swamp milkweed and high-bush blueberry larval food—Dutchman's pipe	marshes near woods along rivers and marshes
zebra swallowtail	adult nectar—highbush blueberry and swamp milkweed larval food—pawpaw	moist woods along rivers and marshes
Hackberry Family		
tawny emperor	adult food—rotting fruit, dung, carrion	dense riverside woods, wooded streams
hackberry emperor	adult food—rotting fruit, dung, carrion	dense riverside woods, wooded streams
Whites and Sulphurs		
cabbage whites	larval food—mustard family, e.g., cabbage, broccoli, etc.	marshes and open areas
falcate orangetip	larval food—rock cress, shepherd's purse	wet open woods, along streams, open swamps
Satyrs and Wood Nymphs		
northern pearly-eye	larval food—white grass and bottlebrush	damp deciduous woods, near streams or marshes
Appalachian eyed brown	larval food—sedges	wet, wooded swamps, shrub swamp
Milkweed Butterflies		
monarch	adult food—milkweed	marshes and other wet places
Skippers		
Peck's skipper	adult food—New York ironweed nectar only	wet meadows near streams and marshes

Butterfly	Food Source	Location
Skippers, continued		
Horace's duskywing	adult food—buttonbush nectar	wooded swamps
tawny-edged skipper	larval food—panic grass adult food—New York ironweed nectar only	wet meadows
Delaware skipper	larval food—grasses adult food—New York ironweed nectar only	damp or wet fields and marshes
dun skipper	larval food—sedges adult food—common milkweed	wet areas near deciduous woods or streams
Gossamer Wing		
harvester	larval food—carnivorous on woolly aphid nymphs	woodlands near slow-moving or swampy streams
bronze copper	adult food—nectar of Indian hemp	open areas near marshes and wet meadows and seeps
striped hairstreak	larval food—N.J. tea, woody plants in rose family	swamps, marsh edges
Brushfoots		
silver-bordered fritillary	larval host—violets adult—spearmint nectar	tall, weedy wet meadows and marshes
meadow fritillary	same as above	same as above
Baltimore checkerspot	adult nectar—daisies	marsh interiors
questionmark	adult—rotting fruits larval food—hackberry	river woods, wooded swamps
mourning cloak	adults—rotting fruits, sap	stream courses, swamp forests
viceroy	larval food—willow leaves	stream and swampy areas, edges of lakes

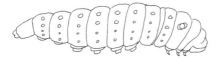

smooth:
tiger swallowtail, 2 inches

smooth with knobs:
viceroy, 1¼ inches

smooth with fleshy filaments:
monarch, 2¾ inches

sluglike:
harvester, ½ inch

branched spines:
mourning cloak, 2½ inches

All butterfly larvae are caterpillars, although they vary in size, color, and pattern.

Observing a Chrysalis. If you want to find a chrysalis, you will have to search on or near the plants that feed the butterfly larvae. The monarch butterfly chrysalis on milkweed plants is probably the most easily found. Near the end of this stage, the opaque chrysalis becomes transparent, and you may be able to see features of the butterfly within. The time spent as a chrysalis varies among species, as does chrysalis design.

EXPLORATIONS

Creating a Butterfly Garden. Pesticides and habitat destruction have made life extremely difficult for butterflies. By planting a garden with wildflowers and shrubs that attract butterflies, you will be helping them while

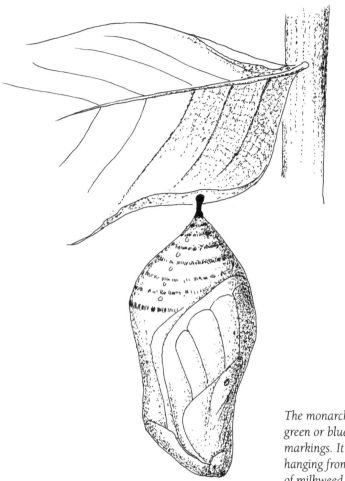

The monarch chrysalis is green or blue with gold markings. It can be found hanging from the leaves of milkweed.

getting an opportunity to enjoy their beauty. The garden does not need to be large. You can add plants that will attract butterflies to an existing garden, or you can use patio containers or flower boxes. To learn what plants attract butterflies in your area, visit public gardens, fields, meadows, and other sunny places during the flowering season. Field guides, botanical gardens, university botany and entomology departments, university extension services, and the people at local nurseries can help you find out more about plants butterflies love. Some plants that attract butterflies are lilac, rhododendron, honeysuckle, butterfly bush, buttonbush, bee balm, daisies, dandelion, hawkweed, Queen Ann's lace, thistle, yarrow, aster, joe-pye weed, ironweed, and willow, plum, and cherry trees.

Raising Butterflies. If you would like to raise butterflies, Carolina Biological Supply can help you get started. Write to Carolina Biological Supply Company, 2700 York Rd., Burlington, NC 27215, or call (919) 584-0381.

Annual Butterfly Count. The North American Butterfly Association (NABA) sponsors an annual butterfly count, usually early in July. You do not have to be an expert to join in this very informative experience; butterfly watchers of all levels and abilities are welcome. NABA also publishes a journal and promotes butterfly photography, field identification, gardening, and conservation. Contact North American Butterfly Association, 4 Delaware Rd., Morristown, NJ 07960, telephone (973) 285-0907, website www.naba.org.

Other Organizations to Join

The Xerces Society, 4828 SE Hawthorne Blvd., Portland, OR 97215

The Lepidopterists Society, Assistant Treasurer, 9417 Carvalho Ct., Bakersfield, CA 93311-1846

Washington Area Butterfly Club, 23 Logan Circle, NW, Washington, DC, 20005, website www.vais.net/butterfly.

CHAPTER 7

Salamanders

APPALACHIAN TREASURES

It was a warm summer night in the sparsely populated Monongahela National Forest. The Appalachian sky was without stars or moon. The dark air was heavy with wetness, and the heat of the day lingered. The forest floor, damp from the drizzle that had fallen hours earlier, was still soft and soggy, and mats of moss, decaying twigs, and other litter contributed to the earthy smells that filled the air. Sandstone boulders and tree trunks dotted with lichen lined the forest trails. Dead leaves stuck together with the glue of heat and water lay across the forest floor and provided shelter for the tiny creatures that made their home in these woodlands. Although this forest is about a hundred miles south of Washington, D.C., even in midsummer it is relatively cool because the altitude is between two thousand and four thousand feet above sea level.

On this night, like a small band of detectives armed with flashlights and plastic collecting dishes, we slowly worked our way along the park trail, carefully stepping over exposed tree roots and shallow puddles in pursuit of an elusive prey. Beams of light guided the search along the ground and under rhododendron thickets and low-growing shrubs bordering the path. Shortly after we began the hunt, there was a soft, yet excited cry of discovery. We quickly gathered at the place where several light beams converged upon the find: a slimy salamander (*Plethodon glutinosus glutinosus*) that measured about six inches long.

Behind this unattractive name is a lovely creature. Its moist, black skin, mottled with white markings, glistened in the artificial light. The salamander tried to scurry away, but our leader caught it and held it in his gentle grasp for a short time as we admired it and learned of its unique features. When released in the place where it was found, the salamander resumed its briefly interrupted hunt for insects.

We continued to explore the area for different kinds of salamanders. We looked into crevices in the sandstone boulders and in nooks and crannies between the irregularly shaped boulders and the ground. We gently pushed aside twigs and fallen leaves. We were not disappointed. Our search yielded the mountain dusky salamander (*Desmognathus ochrophaeus*), the Wehrle's salamander (*Plethodon wehrlei*), and the Cheat Mountain salamander (*Plethodon nettingi*).

Finding the Cheat Mountain salamander was especially rewarding, since it is presently designated as threatened by the U.S. Fish and Wildlife Service. During the last one hundred years, timber harvesting and coal mining have destroyed much of the habit of this three-inch-long amphibian. Since 1976, herpetologists have studied the effects of these radical changes on the life of this salamander. Tree loss and subsequent burning of many areas led to other critical changes in the salamander habitat, destroying the leaf litter and the populations of bryophytes, or mosses and liverworts, that protected the soil from the sun's parching rays. This resulted in an increase in the soil temperature and a decrease in soil moisture. Coal mining also severely altered the habitat. The sides and tops of mountains were sometimes removed, leaving dry, forested islands above high cliff walls, hostile environments where the moisture-requiring salamander could no longer survive. These factors combined to drive the Cheat Mountain salamander into the wetter, cooler habitats found at higher elevations.

When the forest grew back, the area was less moist and not as cool as it had been. The red-backed and mountain dusky salamanders took advantage of these new conditions by filling the niche vacated by the Cheat Mountain salamander. Over a period of many years, these newcomers have done well in that habitat.

There are more salamanders in the Appalachian Mountain region than there are birds and mammals combined. Thus it is an excellent place to study the effects of human activity on them, and the life cycles of various salamander species are being examined in the national forests of western North Carolina. Lumbering is the major industry in the area, and wildlife biologists have discovered that clear-cutting of forests is a significant threat to salamanders, reducing the population of salamanders by about 14 million each year.

Wildlife biologists also fear that the number of black-backed salamanders (*Desmognathus quadramaculatus*) has been adversely affected by bait collectors, who hunt them to provide sport for visiting anglers. To be consistent with the catch-and-release practice used by conservation-minded anglers, artificial lures would be effective replacements for the salamanders.

The beleaguered salamanders also have had to contend with pollution problems. Agricultural pesticides often contaminate the streams and ponds where salamanders live and breed. In the Northwest, ozone depletion has caused increased ultraviolet radiation, which damages egg masses floating in pools and ponds. And acid rain from industrial pollution has made the water that seeps into ponds, streams, and wetlands too acidic for some salamander life.

Each of these environmental changes causes some damage to plant and animal life, but these changes can be disastrous for salamanders, which get most of their essential oxygen not by breathing it into their lungs, but by absorbing it from water or, in the case of terrestrial species, through their moist skin. Water, unless it is stagnant, contains dissolved oxygen. The damp leaf litter, rocky crevices, streambeds, and soggy soils salamanders inhabit all contain life-giving oxygen. Salamanders are efficiently designed for removing this dissolved oxygen from the water that moistens their environments through their skin. This is why they need a moist environment and why they are extremely sensitive to pollution. Many man-made chemicals dissolve in water and are absorbed by the salamanders.

Herpetologists have been concerned for decades about the health of salamanders in various locations throughout their ranges. From North America to Europe, to India, to Costa Rica, salamander populations are experiencing significant declines.

Salamanders are amphibians, and they share membership in this group with frogs and toads. Amphibians were the first animals with backbones (Chordates) to become adapted to life on land some 360 million years ago. Fossil evidence tells us these early amphibians looked much like fish, and they probably lived much like fish for millions of years. Modern amphibians, however, have legs rather than fins and have become less water dependent than their ancestors. Some of today's adult salamanders are land based throughout their entire life.

The life cycle of salamanders is similar to that of frogs: egg, larva (tadpole), and adult. The details of the life cycle vary greatly among species, beginning at courtship, which in some salamander species involves complicated behaviors that may include nose rubbing, hugging, tail waving, and other gentle maneuverings. Spotted salamanders and tiger salamanders have a courtship dance. Marbled salamanders engage in simple body posturing. Red-backed salamanders engage in touching behaviors and tail waving.

Egg-laying practices are just as varied. Some species, such as the spotted salamander, deposit their eggs in large clusters that consist of a mass of black eggs surrounded by a glob of jellylike material. Some newts, semiaquatic salamanders, deposit single, elliptical eggs that cling to underwater plant life. The eggs of the two-lined salamander hang from the undersides of stones, logs, or other objects in moving water. The hellbender, a strictly aquatic salamander, deposits long strands of beadlike eggs that are fiercely guarded by the male in the territory he established earlier in the breeding season. In other species, it is the females that guard the egg clusters, but once the young emerge, they must fend for themselves. Some types of salamanders lay eggs in moist locations where the young with gills can reach water quickly after emerging. In other species, the young leave the eggs as free-swimming tadpoles that closely resemble those of frogs.

Not all salamanders live in water. The red-backed salamander (*Plethodon cinereus*) and some others that belong to the same genus don't live in water at any stage. The larval, or tadpole, stage of these salamanders is completed inside the egg, and the hatchlings are tiny versions of adults.

In the often rough world in which they live, salamanders frequently lose part of an arm or leg. If a forelimb is severed between the elbow and wrist, the remaining limb regenerates the missing part, including the wrist and fingers, in a few months. A similar process occurs if a salamander loses its tail in a struggle with a predator.

Life is difficult for all living things, including salamanders, which must cope with a variety of challenges. Unfortunately, the most threatening challenges can be traced to our continued lack of understanding, our misuse of the environment, and perhaps worst of all, our unwillingness to heed the silent signs of trouble. You have only to read newspapers and magazines at your local library or search the Internet to get the disturbing information. This is a good reason for you to get out and meet a salamander. They need all the friends and advocates they can get.

THE WORLD OF SALAMANDERS

What you will need	Science skills
basic kit	observing
scoop net	recording
large Ziploc bag	measuring
patience	identifying

OBSERVATIONS

Where and When to Find Salamanders. The temperate zone of North America is home to more salamanders than any other continent. Here, salamanders are found primarily in the Appalachian Mountains in the East and along the West Coast. There are too many parks to list all of those that might be home to salamanders. A few parks where there have been successful salamander searches include New River Gorge National River, West Virginia; Great Smoky National Park, Tennessee; Shenandoah National Park, Virginia; Monongahela National Forest, West Virginia; George Washington National Forest and Jefferson National Forest, West Virginia and Virginia; Allegheny National Forest, Pennsylvania; Daniel Boone National Forest, Kentucky; Wayne National Forest, Ohio; Blackwater State Park, West Virginia; Holly River State Park, West Virginia; and Allegheny State Park, New York.

The best time to hunt for salamanders is under cover of darkness because, with the exception of the red eft, they are most active at night. Use your flashlight to comb the ground and along the banks of rivers and streams. You can expect to find them in clumps of moss and other low-growing vegetation such as ferns. At night, it is not necessary to look under rocks, in the cracks of rotting logs, and under patches of loose bark, but during the day, they seek shelter here. Examine leaf litter, and check the wet crevices of rocky ledges.

You may find larvae and adults of some salamanders among the gravel and rocks on the bottoms of clean pools in shallow, moving water. With an aquarium net and tea strainers, you can explore the edges of lakes and bogs. Interesting discoveries await you.

Taking a Closer Look. Is the salamander the same color on its back as it is on the underside? Is the color uniform? If not, describe the pattern of coloration. Are there spots or stripes? What color are they? Where are these markings located? If there are stripes, do they have scalloped edges?

Is the tail as long as the head and body combined? Is it round? Is it flat along the side? Does it have the same pattern and color as the body? How does it help the salamander move? When the salamander crawls, does the tail drag along behind or is it held in the air?

As you become acquainted with different salamanders, keep a record of each in your notebook. Record the size, colors, patterns, number of toes on front and hind feet, where you found them, and a description of the habitat. To find out which family each belongs to, use the outline under "Salamander Identification," below.

The Gait. Although salamanders can scurry through leaf litter to avoid danger, they usually walk slowly enough for you to make some observations. Do they move one foot at a time? Do they use the feet on one side of the body and then those on the other side? What is the job of the hind feet? The front feet? Record your observations, then compare your findings with the pattern described below.

A salamander moves its legs in an alternate and opposite pattern. This means that as the right front foot moves forward, the left hind foot presses against the ground, pushing the body forward. The left front foot is in position to push the salamander forward while the right hind foot gets in position to push the body forward. This pattern of moving causes the body to wiggle from side to side. Watch a human baby crawl and you will see the same pattern.

Sight and Sound. Salamanders do not hear well, but they are able to detect our presence and that of other predators by the vibrations our steps send through the ground as we walk in their habitat. How close can you get to one before it scurries away? This distance is often called the fright distance.

Salamander Identification. The world of salamanders is beautifully diverse. There are about four hundred species worldwide, excluding the Arctic and the Antarctic. Nine families (Ambystomatidae, Amphiumidae, Crypto-branchidae, Dicamptodontidae, Plethodontidae, Proteida, Rhyacotritonidae, Salamandridae, and Sirenidae) reside in North America. Dicamptodontidae and Rhyacotritonidae live west of the Rocky Mountains; the others are found east of the Rockies.

Some salamanders, especially the spotted salamander and the hellbender, are not difficult to recognize by sight, but that is not the case for many others. To check for their special traits, you will need to have the creatures in your hand or held securely in a plastic container or Ziploc bag.

Some of the distinguishing characteristics of salamanders are found on their hind feet and the grooves along the sides of their bodies. For more information about these features, consult one of the field guides listed at the end of this chapter. The outline below identifies the five major families that you are most likely to find. Salamanders that belong to each family are then identified according to their genus and species.

1. Hellbenders (family Cryptobranchidae). The eastern hellbender (*Cryptobranchus alleganiensis*) is the only member of this family, although two subspecies have been identified. These salamanders are unique because of their size.

    Length: 12 to 30 inches.

    Where to look: Under large, flat rocks in clear, swift-moving streams with rocky bottoms.

    What to look for: Stocky, large, gray or brown body. Loose, wrinkled skin along both sides between front and hind legs, which adds oxygen-absorbing surface. Large, easily seen gill slit. Broad, flat head. Uses broad, flat tail and not feet for swimming. Front feet each have four toes, hind feet five.

    Food: Crayfish, shellfish, worms, insect larvae. Trout feed on hellbender larvae and small adults.

2. Mud puppies or water dogs (family Proteidae). These salamanders are very large, but only half the size of the hellbenders.

    Length: 8 to 17 inches.

    Where to look: Permanent weedy ponds, lakes, streams, and rivers, where they hide under rocks, logs, and other debris; bank overhangs are good hiding places, too.

Range of the eastern hellbender (Cryptobranchus alleganiensis)

The hellbender, a strictly aquatic salamander, is almost always found in clear-flowing rivers and streams with rocky bottoms. Length 12 to 30 inches.

Range of the mud puppy (Necturus maculosus)

Mud puppies are particularly well camouflaged among leaf litter and gravel in ponds or river bottoms. Look for dark red gills behind the head. Length 8 to 17 inches.

What to look for: External bushy gills throughout its life. Four toes on each of four well-developed feet. Flat head with swelling behind small lidless eyes. Rusty brown back with irregular black spots, undersides gray.

Food: Fish eggs, crayfish, and insects.

3. Newts (family Salamandridae). The red-spotted newt (red eft) (*Notophthalmus viridescens*) is the only member of the family.

Length: 2½ to 5½ inches.

Where to look: A wide range of watery habitats, especially quiet pools, ponds, and swamps, where mature adults may be seen floating near the water's surface. If temporary ponds dry up, they burrow into mud until water returns. Immature stage, called red eft, wanders the woodland floor until mature (three to seven years).

Range of red-spotted newt (Notophthalmus viridescens viridescens)

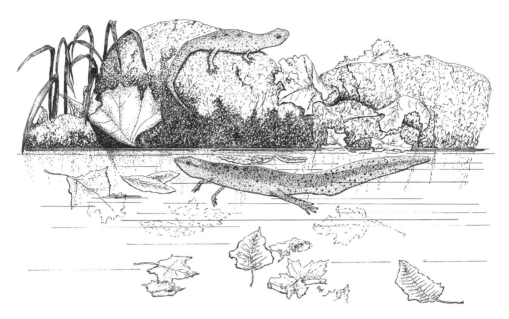

The red-spotted newt changes from orange-red to dark olive as it matures and moves back into the water. Both stages have red dots encircled in black in a line along the sides. Length 2½ to 5½ inches.

What to look for: Immature stage (eft) noted for its rough, bright, red-orange skin. The back of waterbound adult is greenish brown with black dots, and a line of black-bordered red dots along its side. Its yellow belly has a scattering of small, black spots.

Food: Worms, insect larvae, crustaceans, slugs, and snails.

4. Mole salamanders (family Ambystomatidae)

a. Spotted salamander (*Ambystoma maculatum*)

Length: 5½ to 8 inches.

Where to look: Deciduous woodlands, where they wander on the forest floor during rainy nights. Look under logs and heaps of soggy leaves, in freshly plowed fields, and even in damp trash heaps.

What to look for: Stout, slate-colored, or black body with two irregular rows of orange or yellow spots from head to tail. Gray undersides.

Food: Earthworms, snails, slugs, pill bugs, crustaceans, and insects and their larvae.

Range of the spotted salamander (Ambystoma maculatum)

*a. The spotted salamander,
length 5½ to 8 inches.*

*b. The marbled salamander,
length 3½ to 5 inches.*

Most salamanders are rarely found walking on the surface of the ground, so you'll have to turn over rocks, logs, and debris to find them.

Range of the marbled salamander (Ambystoma opacum)

b. Marbled salamander (*Ambystoma opacum*)

　Length: 3½ to 5 inches

　Where to look: Wet deciduous woodlands, swamp borders, flood-plains, and streambanks. Look under wet leaves, logs, and trash.

　What to look for: Stocky body with alternating black and silvery (males) or grayish (females) bands on back. Slow moving; don't scurry away from flashlight beam the way many other salamanders do.

　Food: Earthworms, insects, snails, slugs, crustaceans, and spiders.

5. Lungless salamanders (family Plethodontidae)

a. Dusky salamanders (*Desmognathus* sp.)

　Northern dusky salamander (*Desmognathus fuscus fuscus*)

　　Length: 2½ to 5½ inches.

　　Where to look: Very damp areas that border streams and brooks, where they hide during the day under damp leaves, logs, and rocks.

Range of the northern dusky salamander (Desmognathus fuscus fuscus)

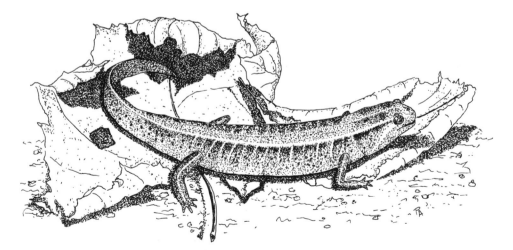

The markings on the northern dusky salamander are extremely variable, making them difficult to identify. Look for them in very damp areas that border streams. Length 2½ to 5½ inches.

What to look for: Robust brown or clay-colored body, mottled with dark spots that fuse to a wavy line on each side of the back. Light line from eye to angle of jaw. Hard for the beginner to identify, but it can be done by eliminating known species. This salamander is agile and difficult to capture for field observation.

Food: Earthworms, snails, slugs, soft-bodied insects, mites, and spiders.

b. Woodland salamanders (*Plethodon* sp.)

1. Red-backed salamander (*Plethodon cinereus*)

Length: 2½ to 5 inches.

Where to look: Moist deciduous, coniferous, and mixed woodlands, where it hides under bark, logs, leaves, and rocks.

What to look for: Small, slender body with straight-edged red to orange line down the back, sometimes extending to tip of tail. Round tail, not keel shaped. Sides and belly lead gray. There is also a lead-backed phase that lacks the red to orange stripe.

Food: Snails, earthworms, spiders, millipedes, insect larvae, and ants.

Range of the red-backed salamander (Plethodon cinereus cinereus)

The red-backed salamander is a terrestrial salamander confined to wooded or forested areas, where it hides beneath all kinds of objects, including trash. Length 2½ to 5 inches.

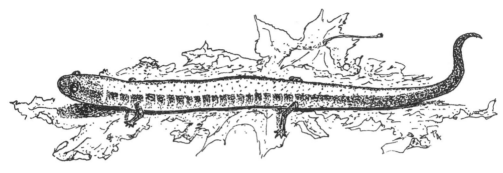

2. Slimy salamander *(Plethodon glutinosus glutinosus)*

   Length: 4½ to 8 inches.

   What to look for: Shiny black back, sprinkled generously with white flecks that have brass-colored accents. Throat and undersides slate gray.

   Where to look: Moist ravines, wooded floodplains, and under stacks of moist leaves.

   Food: Spiders, mites, millipedes, earthworms, insects, and snails.

c. Four-toed salamanders *(Hemidactylium* sp.)

   Four-toed salamander *(Hemidactylium scutatum)*. The only member of the genus.

   Length: 2 to 4 inches.

   Where to look: In hardwood forests under logs, piles of leaves, and stones. Females relatively easy to locate on nests at the edges of ponds and small streams, in fens and other wetlands. However, they should not be disturbed, especially at this time.

   What to look for: Rusty brown back and white undersides, with black speckles that extend to the tail. Four toes on hind feet. Tail constricted at base. When exposed, adult quickly forms a tight coil with its back side up; in this position, its rust-brown color blends with the leaf litter. Under stress or if captured by the tail, the salamander can separate from it.

Range of the slimy salamander (Plethodon glutinosus glutinosus)

The slimy salamander is the "stick" salamander. Its skin gland secretions cling to your hands like glue and almost always have to wear off. Length 4½ to 8 inches.

Range of the four-toed salamander (Hemidactylium scutatum)

The tail of the four-toed salamander breaks off easily at its grooved base. When this happens, a new tail quickly grows to replace it. Length 2 to 4 inches.

    d. Red salamanders (*Pseudotriton* sp.)

        Northern red salamander *(Pseudotriton ruber ruber)*

            Length: 3½ to 6 inches.

            What to look for: Stout body with fleshy tail. Young salamanders bright red but adults become dark or cloudy red. Black dots on the back in youth and maturity. Yellow eye iris.

Range of the red salamander (Pseudotriton ruber ruber)

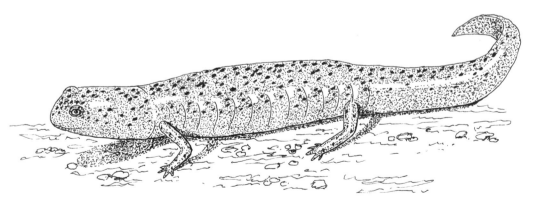

The red salamander is often found in or near springs and streams. It can be found in rivulets if the water is clear, cool, and not stagnant. Length 3½ to 6 inches.

Where to look: Under logs, stones, mosses, and heaps of damp leaves by small streams. Relatively common in fens and bogs. Active at night. May be seen on roadways in spring.

Food: Spiders, slugs, insects, earthworms, and smaller salamanders.

e. Brook salamanders (*Eurycea* sp.)

Northern two-lined salamander *(Eurycea bislineata bislineata)*

Length: May reach 4 inches.

What to look for: Slender and small body with back varying from dull green-yellow to bright orange-yellow or light brown. Light stripe down the back onto the tail, bordered by dark lines extending from each eye. Stripe may be dotted with black flecks. Sides, legs, and undersides yellow or yellow-orange.

Where to look: Along streamsides under rocks, logs, or leaves.

When to look: May be found year-round. They find warmth under snow in snowy regions; remove snow cover and rake away leaves.

Food: Mites, beetles, flies, and springtails.

Range of the northern two-lined salamander (Eurycea bislineata bislineata)

The two-lined salamander is essentially a brookside salamander, although in warm, wet weather, it may wander far out into nearby woodlands. Length 2½ to 4 inches.

REFERENCES

Conant, Roger, and Joseph Collins. *Peterson Field Guide to Reptiles and Amphibians of Eastern/Central North America.* New York: Houghton Mifflin, 1998.

Green, N. Bayard, and Thomas K. Pauley. *Amphibians and Reptiles in West Virginia.* Pittsburgh, PA: University of Pittsburgh Press, 1987.

Malcolm, L. Hunter, Jr., John Albright, and Jane Arbuckle, eds. *The Amphibians and Reptiles of Maine.* Orno, ME: Maine Agricultural Experiment Station, University of Maine, 1992.

Martof, Bernard S., William M. Palmer, Joseph R. Bailey, and Julian R. Harrison III. *Amphibians and Reptiles of the Carolinas and Virginia.* Chapel Hill, NC: The University of North Carolina Press, 1980.

Petranka, James W. *Salamanders of the United States and Canada.* Washington, DC: Smithsonian Institution Press, 1998.

Pfingsten, Ralph A., and Floyd L. Downs, eds. *Salamanders of Ohio.* Columbus, OH: College of Biological Sciences, Ohio State University, 1989.

CHAPTER 8

Frogs

NIGHT VOICES THAT PROCLAIM SPRING

If you were to ask some friends how they knew that spring had finally arrived, they would probably list melting snow, greening grass, budding trees, and calling birds. Some might also note such nocturnal signs as the nasal *peent* of the woodcock or the song of the cricket. Others would insist that the true herald of spring is the bell-like sound of spring peepers (*Hyla crucifer* or *Pseudacris crucifer*) rising out of the wetlands. As they have done for millions of years, spring peepers and other frogs raise their voices to proclaim the start of breeding season—spring.

Frogs were among the first vertebrates (animals with backbones) capable of spending their adult lives on land. Although their lineage is not clear, it can be traced back to a primitive fish called ichthyostegalia. Somewhere along the evolutionary path, descendants of this fish surrendered many of the characteristics that tied them to the sea. The fossil record does not give the exact time and nature of that transformation; however, the fossils do show that those early frogs shared the world of the steamy early Jurassic forests with plants, dinosaurs, and invertebrates such as scorpions, spiders, and various flying insects.

Today, there are 3,800 known species of frogs worldwide, 82 of which live in North America. Frogs are amphibians, which means that in the course of their lifespan they lead a "double life," first in water and then on land. As eggs and larvae they are bound to a watery existence in freshwater ponds, streams, lakes, or even puddles, but then as adults they adapt to life on land. Scientists place frogs in a special group of amphibians called *anurans*. The word means "without tail" and distinguishes frogs from salamanders and caecilians.

There is nothing like a warm, rainy April night to start frogs calling in their many voices. In early spring we hear males making "advertisement calls" as they define territorial boundaries and alert females to their presence. "Aggressive calls" are made when a male frog spies another male trespassing in his territory. Such intrusions are generally settled peacefully, with the intruder hopping off unharmed. Once territories have been established and females have arrived, the males sing their "courtship calls." If you live close to some pristine wetlands, listen for these three types of calls, as well as the calls of various frog species. Individual frogs can be identified by slight differences in their voices, but this requires very careful listening over a period of time.

Once a female frog has selected her mate from a chorus of competing males, the two join in an embrace called *amplexus,* in which the male grabs

Having found a mate, the male frog grasps her behind her forelimbs, enabling him to fertilize the eggs as they are laid. This embrace is called amplexus.

the female with his forelegs and hooks his thumbs under her front legs. While in this position the female lays her eggs, and the male releases huge quantities of sperm into the water. This process, called external fertilization, may seem rather haphazard, but it has been extremely successful in producing continuous generations of frogs.

You are likely to hear a breeding pond before you see it; it will resound with splashing water and grunting, squawking, hiccupping, yelping, kicking, and squirming frogs. In the confusion, a male frog sometimes embraces something other than a willing female and one of the frogs will sound the alarm in the form of a "release call." There is so much bedlam in a breeding pond that male frogs have been known to hug almost anything that moves, even a human hand.

Once successful breeding has occurred, fertilized eggs are deposited in safe places, which vary according to the species of frog. For example, the eastern spadefoot toad prefers to deposit its eggs in small ponds created by torrential rains. It doesn't matter that these ponds evaporate quickly because it takes only two weeks for the eggs to develop into toads. Bullfrogs (*Rana catesbeiana*) choose more permanent bodies of water, and green frogs (*Rana clamitans*) live in bogs, swamps, and marshes. Frogs usually deposit their eggs in clusters, and toads lay single or double strands of eggs. Look for these long strands in the vegetation along the shallows of permanent ponds or lakes.

A single frog can produce huge quantities of eggs. Gray tree frogs (*Hyla*

Frog eggs are found in clumps; toad eggs, in strands.

versicolor) lay about 2,000 eggs in small, mucus-coated packets, with 6 to 45 eggs in each packet. The American toad (*Bufo americanus*) deposits between 2,000 and 9,000 eggs in double strands a few feet long. Another variation in egg laying is illustrated by the bullfrog, which lays between 10,000 and 20,000 eggs in a gigantic gelatinous envelope that can spread two to four feet across the water's surface. Mucus covers the two envelopes that protect each of the 1,000 to 3,000 eggs laid by the green frog. Because frog eggs are so vulnerable, most of the eggs and larvae are devoured by predators such as fish, other tadpoles, small mammals, snakes, wading birds, and insects.

Young frogs hatch from their eggs as tadpoles. Generally speaking, neither eggs nor tadpoles are dependent on parental care, so adult frogs are free from the tasks of brooding eggs and feeding the young. Tadpoles survive by exploiting the energy-rich environment of the pond, puddle, or roadside ditch where they live. As they swim, their movement stirs up decaying plant material from the bottom of the pond, nutritious food for hungry tadpoles. The tadpoles' diet helps to extend the life of the pond by cleaning it: without the tadpoles to eat this plant matter, the bacteria of decay would deplete the pond water of oxygen. A pond without oxygen cannot support life-forms; it is dead.

Tadpoles have very large heads, necessary to house the complex filtering system used to strain food from the water. This system acts as a pump, regulating the amount of water that enters the tadpole's mouth. If the pond water is dense with food, a smaller amount of water is admitted, much like a person will take in a larger mouthful of broth than of thick stew. The filtering mechanism enables tadpoles to live in water so turbid that you cannot see them or in a pond so clear that the water looks empty of food.

The length of the tadpole phase varies with frog species and environmental factors. Within a species, the time spent as a tadpole also can vary with geographic location and water temperature. For example, spring peeper tadpoles take as long as 90 to 100 days to develop in the northern part of their range, but tadpoles of the same species living in Florida will become frogs in as little as 45 days. Scientists studying the larvae of green frogs developing in the ponds of Michigan discovered that these tadpoles show a similar response to environmental temperature. The tadpoles that hatched from eggs deposited early in the season became frogs in about 80 days, but those developing from eggs laid later in the summer generally stopped growing when the cold weather arrived and sought the warmth of the pond mud, where they spent the winter. The tadpole stage for this group could last as long as 360 days. A tailed frog (*Ascaphus truei*) living in the northwestern United States holds the record at 1,080 days in tadpole stage.

Some frogs live for as long as nine years, but most live about four. Therefore, frogs living in cold climates need some strategies for surviving the winter. American and spadefoot toads sleep in burrows beneath the earth; wood frogs and gray tree frogs (*Hyla versicolor*) prefer to overwinter on the forest

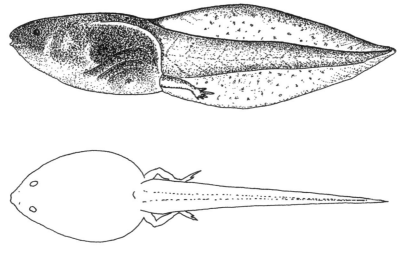

Wood frog tadpole
(Rana sylvatica)

Life cycle of a frog

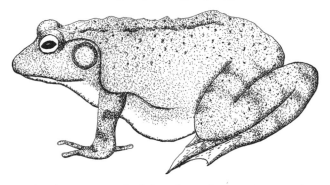

6. The plant-eating tadpole has changed into an insect-eating frog—an adult capable of reproducing.

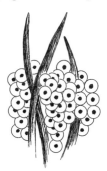

1. The female lays soft, jelly-covered eggs in the water of a pond, and they are fertilized by the male.

5. Gills are replaced with lungs; the mouth and eyes change and the tail is absorbed.

2. A tiny, fishlike tadpole hatches from an egg.

3. The tadpole breathes through feathery gills that grow on each side of the head. These quickly disappear, to be replaced by internal gills.

4. The hind legs grow first. The front legs grow under the skin and then break through.

floor or in rock crevices covered by leaf litter. Green frogs find shelter on the bottoms of ponds, lakes, or streams, whereas northern leopard frogs snuggle into the soft ooze of streambeds, lakes, and ponds. Scientists know a great deal about the breeding life of many frog species but little about the way they spend the rest of their year.

The life cycle of frogs is called *complete metamorphosis*, which means they pass through egg, larva (tadpole), and adult phases. During the egg and larva stages, they are dependent on water. Some frog species, however, lay their eggs on the ground and do not pass through a water-dependent tadpole stage. Some scientists believe that these species illustrate stages in evolutionary development from water-dependent creatures to those that are completely land dwellers. They estimate that every major frog family has some of these rebellious members that no longer deposit their eggs in the water or produce tadpoles. Instead, small frogs of the species hatch directly from the eggs. The life cycle of these frogs more closely resembles the incomplete metamorphoses of crickets and grasshoppers than that of their anuran cousins. Don't expect to find these rebels in your local pond, though—they live in the tropics where they are not subject to the stresses associated with seasonal change.

Adult frogs must live near water to reproduce, thus water remains essential to the success of the species. During the breeding season they need to mate and deposit their eggs in water because frog eggs are wrapped in a gelatin-like material that easily dries out, rather than a calcium case or leathery shell like bird or turtle eggs.

Although most adult frogs do not drink, all frogs absorb water through their permeable skins, especially the abdominal skin. Some frogs sit for some time during the day in small puddles to replace the water lost through their skin or used in metabolism. Frogs of one species counter water loss by secreting a waxy substance and rubbing it on themselves. Tree frogs have evolved another strategy: They spend the hottest part of the day with their abdomens pressed against the bark of a tree, which minimizes water loss through their permeable abdominal skin. It could be that the problem of water loss is a factor in making frogs creatures of the night, because the night is cooler and more moist. The daytime sun can make it dangerous for frogs to be out.

Herpetologists—those who study the life and times of frogs—are becoming more and more concerned about the amphibians' future. The reports from 1989 and 1990 conferences held by the World Congress of Herpetology and by the Biology Board of the National Research Council cite an alarming worldwide decline in some frog species. Though scientists agree that frogs have had to cope with predators and variations in rainfall, they point out that

Pacific tree frog
(Hyla regilla)

because frogs absorb moisture through their skin, they are susceptible to pollutants dissolved in the water such as insecticides and pesticides. These chemicals are leached from the land as rain and melting snow drain into frog breeding ponds. Frogs are also gravely affected by acid rain. Habitat destruction through the draining of wetlands for homes and agriculture by humans is another cause of their decreasing numbers, and frogs are killed by cars, generally on roads that separate breeding pools from winter resting places.

Frog voices calling from bogs and swamps as soft rains fall on the still-cold earth stir a sense of hope and of regeneration every spring, but there may come a time when we won't hear those magical sounds. Frogs, like the birds, are warning us that there is a problem with the environment; these beautiful creatures are telling us that something is very wrong in the frog pond.

THE WORLD OF FROGS

What you will need
basic kit
dip net
large Ziploc bag
gallon jar
tape recorder
dedication

Science skills
observing
recording
measuring

OBSERVATIONS

Putting Anurans in Order. People tend to lump all frogs into a few simple categories—pond frogs versus toads, big frogs versus little frogs—but the world of nature is much more complicated than that. Even in the world of the frogs it is beautifully diverse. Scientists have organized frogs into several groups: tailed frogs, narrow-mouthed toads, spadefoot toads, true toads, cricket frogs, chorus frogs, tree frogs, and true frogs. The activities in this chapter focus on a few of the most available frogs in each major group, as follows:

• Spadefoot toads—eastern spadefoot toad *(Scaphiopus holbrooki)*
• True toads—American toad *(Bufo americanus)*
• Tree frogs—spring peeper *(Pseudacris crucifer)*, gray tree frog *(Hyla versicolor)*
• True frogs—eastern wood frog *(Rana sylvatica)*, northern leopard frog *(Rana pipiens)*, green frog *(Rana clamitans)*, bullfrog *(Rana catesbeiana)*

These representative frogs have a wide range east of the Rocky Mountains. You can find other species in your locality by consulting a field guide to amphibians. The specific habitats preferred by these frogs are outlined in the chart that follows.

Frog	Habitat
eastern spadefoot toad *(Scaphiopus holbrooki)*	gravelly, sandy, or loamy soils of dunes, farmlands, forests, and meadows
American toad *(Bufo americanus)*	diverse, dry habitats including meadows, suburban backyards, mountain forests
spring peeper *(Pseudacris crucifer)*	low-growing shrubs near temporary pools and inland wetlands, floodplains
gray tree frog *(Hyla versicolor)*	trees and shrubs near temporary woodland wetlands
eastern wood frog *(Rana sylvatica)*	damp woodlands, shaded wooded hillsides, meadows
northern leopard frog *(Rana pipiens)*	damp meadows, fields, orchards, brackish marshes
green frog *(Rana clamitans)*	wetlands, along the edges of streams and ponds
bullfrog *(Rana catesbeiana)*	permanent bodies of water, ponds, lakes

When Some Frogs Call. The chart below identifies the months when you can expect to hear the breeding calls of some frogs and toads. Listen for the calls of the frogs in your area and make a similar chart for them. If you do this for several seasons you will notice patterns that will help you predict when they will arrive each year. When there are departures from the pattern, you can explore possible explanations such as an extremely cold winter or habitat destruction. Scientists look for patterns in animal behavior and investigate changes. Frequently, records kept by nonprofessionals are helpful in finding trends and causes.

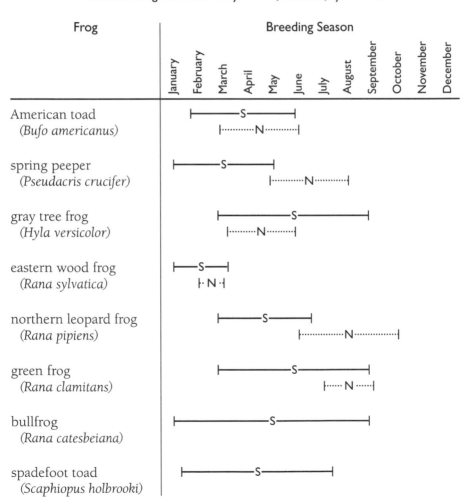

BREEDING CALLS

Southern range is indicated by ⊢S⊣; northern, by ⊢···N···⊣.

Frog	Breeding Season

American toad
(*Bufo americanus*)

spring peeper
(*Pseudacris crucifer*)

gray tree frog
(*Hyla versicolor*)

eastern wood frog
(*Rana sylvatica*)

northern leopard frog
(*Rana pipiens*)

green frog
(*Rana clamitans*)

bullfrog
(*Rana catesbeiana*)

spadefoot toad
(*Scaphiopus holbrooki*)

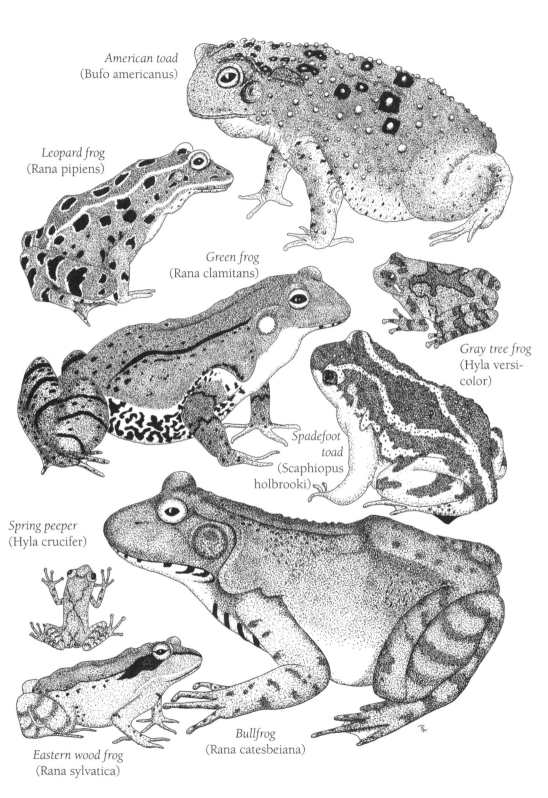

American toad
(Bufo americanus)

Leopard frog
(Rana pipiens)

Green frog
(Rana clamitans)

Gray tree frog
(Hyla versi-
color)

Spadefoot
toad
(Scaphiopus
holbrooki)

Spring peeper
(Hyla crucifer)

Bullfrog
(Rana catesbeiana)

Eastern wood frog
(Rana sylvatica)

Rain and humidity bring out the frogs. If the night is windless, so much the better. Listen early in the spring for the calling that marks the beginning of the frogs' annual trek from winter hideouts to their breeding places. Once this migration begins, you can expect the calling to continue into summer. Throughout this period you may see hundreds of frogs hopping across country roads because these roadways cut through the bogs, swamps, and other inland wetlands frogs use for breeding.

If you are not able to locate any frog ponds, ask the naturalists at a local nature center or museum or contact a local group such as the Audubon Society. Members of your local or regional herpetological society are also excellent resources.

Frog Calls. The most accurate way to identify a frog call is to see the vocalist in action, but this is not always possible. A good substitute is to listen to recordings. With the help of modern technology, scientists have recorded frog calls in the field and you can use these at home. Sometimes your local library will have a tape or will get it if you request it.

The following table describes frog calls as compiled by field investigators. It is very difficult to put animal sounds into print, but perhaps this listing will help you.

FROG CALLS

Frog	Sounds
bullfrog (Rana catesbeiana)	deep hum or drone, "burr woom," "jug-o-rum," "ooohoom"
spadefoot toad (Scaphiopus holbrooki)	deep, explosive, nasal "waank" or "waagh"
green frog (Rana clamitans)	banjolike, explosive single note or a series of plunks descending in scale
spring peeper (Pseudacris crucifer)	whistlelike, high peep, slurred, higher pitch at the end, 1-second intervals
gray tree frog (Hyla versicolor)	brief, hoarse, 2–6 seconds long
American toad (Bufo americanus)	high-pitched and musical, 5–30 seconds, has a distinct flutelike quality
eastern wood frog (Rana sylvatica)	"quack," like a duck
northern leopard frog (Rana pipiens)	snorelike croaks

There are those who say that frog calls lack melody, but all agree that the calls have character. Make a tape recording of frog calls to help you decide. (See Chapter Note 1.)

Sneak Up on a Frog. Frogs will immediately be quiet if they detect your footsteps as you approach their calling area. How close can you get to them before they stop calling? Do they all stop their calling at once? If you wait quietly at the edge of the pond, they will resume their calls. How long does it take for this to happen? Do they all start up together, or do they seem to have a leader? Can you map out the locations of leaders and followers?

To Catch a Frog. You need very little equipment to capture a frog. Your bare hands are very good tools, but you may prefer to use a scoop net. (See Chapter Note 2.) The best resource person you can possibly find is a twelve-year-old who lives near a pond. If you are collecting at night, a flashlight with a strong beam is important. When you have the frog in hand, put it into a Ziploc bag and seal it without removing the air. Be sure to include a damp paper towel in the bag to provide moisture for the frog until you have a chance to observe it.

You will notice that frogs face the water when they sit by the edge of a pond. If you put your net in front of the frog, it will be startled and leap into your net.

Is It a Frog or a Toad? It's easy to tell frogs and toads from other amphibians such as salamanders and newts. What is not so easy is to separate frogs from their closer relatives, the toads, as the terms *frog* and *toad* often cause some confusion. It is easiest to make the distinction if you remember that *frog* is an umbrella term that includes all hopping or leaping amphibians, including toads. In other words, toads are a type of frog. The following are a few guidelines that will help you to decide which creature you've captured.

Did you find the critter in a moist habitat such as a marsh, pond, or swampy area? Is it slim with smooth skin and long slender legs? Does it move quickly and leap great distances (greater than its body length)? Did you find it near others of its kind? If you have answered yes to these questions, you probably have caught a frog.

If you found the animal by itself in a drier habitat, such as woodland, meadow, or suburban yard, and thick, bumpy skin covers its plump body, it's a safe guess that you have captured a toad. Prominent bony ridges on top of their heads (cranial crests) and conspicuous swelling behind their eyes (parotid glands) are other marks of toads.

Toads also are known for their sluggish movements, and with stubby legs they hop rather than leap as frogs do. Some frog species such as the gray tree frog have rough skin, which may lead you to believe they are toads, and other frog species may even look like toads—but their long legs and moist skin are good clues to their identity.

TOAD IDENTIFICATION

American toad (*Bufo americanus*)	large, slow moving reddish brown large red warts one large wart in each spot on back underside spotted with black
common toad (*Bufo woodhousei*)	smaller, more agile greenish gray small dark green warts several warts in each spot underside generally creamy white
spadefoot toad (*Scaphiopus holbrooki*)	no bony crests over eyes small, round parotids conspicuous black, bony "spades" on each hind foot smooth skin

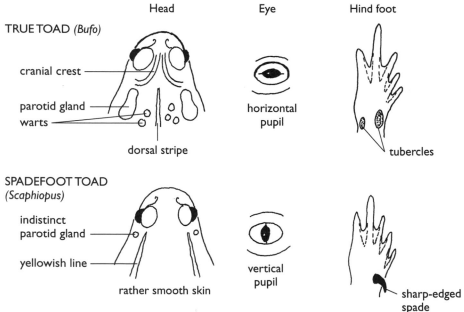

Comparison of the true toad and the spadefoot toad

FROG IDENTIFICATION

TREE FROGS (*Hyla* spp.): Swollen discs on tips of toes, toes not webbed

spring peeper (*H. crucifer*)	has "x" on its back 1 inch long light ash gray to light brown
gray tree frog (*H. versicolor*)	ash gray yellow-white spot below eye rough skin

TRUE FROGS (*Rana* spp.): Seldom found far from water. Many have two ridges (dorsolateral folds) of skin that begin behind the eye and run down on either side of the back. All have webbed toes.

bullfrog (*R. catesbeiana*)	largest frog, 6–8 inches long large mouth color dusky, mottled bars of dark color on legs no dorsolateral folds
green frog (*R. clamitans*)	small leaps widely into water when disturbed, often "screaming" dorsolateral folds bright green head and shoulders shades to dusty brown or olive on back
wood frog (*R. sylvatica*)	small, slender very long hind legs pronounced dorsolateral folds chocolate brown or fawn colored wears a "face mask" spends a lot of time away from water
northern leopard frog (*R. pipiens*)	3–5 inches long hunts insects in grassy meadows eardrum (tympanum) almost size of eye dorsolateral folds head somewhat pointed large light-bordered spots on back

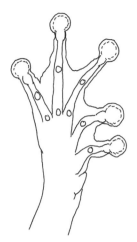

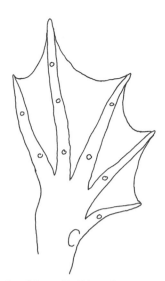

The hind feet of tree frogs have adhesive discs on toes, which help them cling to twigs and bark.

The hind feet of bullfrogs have extensive webs; fourth toe protrudes well beyond other toes.

Additional Observations. Almost everyone knows a frog when he sees one, and even small children can tell us that frogs have bulging eyes, wide mouths, and front legs shorter than their hind legs. What may not be so widely known is the way their tongues work. The long, sticky tongue of a frog is attached at the front of its mouth rather than the back, which allows it to do a remarkable thing. Like a fly fisherman casting his line, the frog can flip its tongue into the air and snare a passing insect with amazing speed and efficiency.

Look closely at the frog's eyes. How does it blink its eyes? Does it have eyelids? (See Chapter Note 3.)

Frogs have eardrums, or tympanic membranes, which are round and often a different color than the frog's skin. Look for them behind the eyes. In some frog species you can distinguish the males from the females by the size of the eardrum relative to the eye. If the eardrum is larger than the eye, the frog is a male; if the eardrum is about the same size as the frog's eye, then the frog is a female.

Look at the area behind the frog's eyes. Do you see a conspicuous swelling behind each eye? These are the parotid glands, which toads use to produce toxic chemicals that are distasteful to predators. When threatened, a toad will lower its head to the level of its abdomen, so that when the predator attacks, it will grab the parotids, thus getting a mouthful of foul-tasting, toxic

The frog has a long, sticky tongue attached to the front of the mouth. When an insect flies by, the frog's tongue is propelled out for an instant to grab it.

chemicals. Some frogs, such as the northern leopard frog, similarly secrete acidic fluids that irritate the mucous lining in the predator's mouth.

What color is your frog? Is the color uniform throughout the frog's body? Are there areas that are light in color and others that are dark? Where is the least amount of color? Where is the most color? What advantage do you think this pattern of coloration or shading has for the frog? (See Chapter Note 4.)

The frog you have caught is beautifully designed for living in the water. How do its legs and feet help it to thrive in that environment? Are all feet equally webbed? Can you think of a reason for this? Do the front feet have the same number of toes as the hind feet?

Spadefoot toads are equipped with a special hard, crescent-shaped spade at the heel of each hind foot, an adaptation the toad uses for digging back-

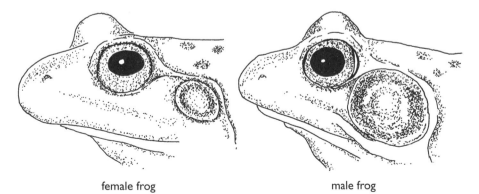

female frog   male frog

Frogs do not have exterior ears. The eardrum lies on the surface behind the frog's eyes. Many times eardrums of males are larger than those of females.

wards into its burrow beneath the sandy soil. Young spadefoot toads must make their burrows in very soft, crumbly soil because their spades are soft.

What is its general body shape? How is this an advantage for a creature that spends a great deal of time in the water?

Compare the frog skeleton with a human skeleton. You will notice that frogs don't have ribs. Look for other differences and similarities.

Getting to Know a Frog. One of the most rewarding aspects of frog watching is that you can learn to identify individuals. This kind of identification is important to scientists because it helps them find out such things about a frog as how far it roams, what its territorial boundaries are, and how long it lives. One investigator discovered that an American toad (*Bufo americanus*) lived in his backyard for nine years.

Although frogs and toads of the same species will look similar to each other, you can learn to recognize individual differences in color and pattern design. With practice you will know whether the frog in the garden on one night is the same frog that appears there on other occasions. To do this, you will need to make careful records of each of the frogs you find. Look carefully and record the pattern of color on each frog that you are observing.

Drawings and close-up photographs are additional tools that will help you discriminate among the individuals you find. Add the illustrations to your permanent field collection.

Herpetologists use a method called *toe clipping* to help them identify individual frogs. This procedure does not cause the frog much distress, and the clipped toe will regenerate. For more information on toe clipping, consult *The Amphibians* by Ray and Patricia Ashton.

Photographing Anurans. To add interest to frog watching, you can photograph your subjects in their natural habitat. Because most frogs are quite small and are active at night, you will need some close-up or telephoto lenses and flash equipment. Taking pictures of frogs requires tremendous patience, but the rewards are great. A staged photograph with a captive animal will add interest to your collection, and photos will enrich your field notes.

Observing Food Chains and Webs. Frogs and toads eat invertebrates. Most of these are insects, but spiders, ants, and even earthworms have a place in the anuran diet. Thus, adult frogs and toads are predators. The prey need to be moving in order to activate the feeding response in frogs. You can observe this if you sit quietly beside a frog pond in the twilight. Watch carefully, and you may witness a frog capture a dragonfly or other large insect with its tongue.

Frogs and toads are also delicacies for many other animals. As you spend time around the frog "hot spots," look for the creatures that prey on them. You may be on hand to see some food chains at work. Some frog predators include skunks, turtles, hognosed snakes, garter snakes, wading birds such as green herons, fish, and small mammals such as weasels, raccoons, and muskrats. Even domestic cats and dogs may help themselves to a frog or two.

While you are observing the food chains that involve frogs, look for those in which tadpoles are among the players. Newts, fish, water beetles, and water scorpions are a few tadpole predators.

Flashlight Hunt. The most productive time to hunt for frogs and toads is after a heavy rain. Because many frogs and toads reflect light from their eyes, they will be easier to find if you hold a flashlight at eye level and shine the beam in the direction of the pond or the frog sounds. You may have seen eye shine of dogs or cats reflected in headlight beams. Perhaps you have seen this phenomenon in photos you have taken of your dog while using a flash-bulb—the dog's eyes appear red. Bullfrogs are especially easy to locate by this method, as their eyes shine an opalescent green. (See Chapter Note 5.)

EXPLORATIONS

Observing Life Cycles. Frogs pass through a complete metamorphosis as they develop. This means that as adults they do not resemble the creatures that hatched from the eggs. You can observe the life cycle of a frog from egg to adult by setting up a simple aquarium and putting some frog eggs in it.

Eggs. Frogs lay their jelly-coated eggs in fresh water. Look for them in a pond, puddle, bog, swamp, or any other wet area where frogs breed. You can even find frog spawn (fertilized eggs) in roadside ditches that have been filled by spring rains. Look for the gelatinous masses often tangled in pond vegetation. The water causes the protective jelly to swell, so it's not unusual to see a mass of frog eggs as large as a football. If you have ever tried to pick them out of the water, you know that spawn is very slippery. The advantage for the frogs is that slippery eggs are not easy for predators to grab. The egg masses of some species have such buoyancy that they will float in water. Some tree frogs (*Hyla* sp.) deposit their tiny eggs singly or in small clusters that are difficult to find.

Toad eggs are covered with waterproof material and laid in long strands, sometimes double strands. Look for them along the shallows of ponds or lakes. (See Chapter Note 6.) If you can watch the development of a frog starting at the egg stage, you can observe a tadpole as it becomes an adult.

If you can find some eggs, scoop up a few and put them into a wide-mouthed container. Three or four eggs are enough. When they hatch you can transfer the tadpoles to a larger container (see below). Because tadpoles are sensitive to chlorine and the iron that leaches from water pipes, be sure to use pond water rather than tap water for your aquarium.

Tadpoles (Larvae). Although you have probably seen tadpoles swimming in ponds, you may not have observed them in an orderly way. Systematic observation is a very different way of seeing. A good way to begin systematic observation is to capture one or two tadpoles and observe their structure and their behavior. You can scoop tadpoles out of the pond with a fine mesh net, available in any shop that sells home aquarium supplies. Wear a pair of old sneakers, as you may need to wade into the water.

After capturing the tadpoles, put them into a large container that allows them to swim freely. A wide-mouthed gallon jar is sufficient for two or three tadpoles. Your enthusiasm may push you to take more, but resist the urge to do so unless you plan to use an air pump and a larger container. Add enough water from the pond where you found the tadpoles so that the jar is about three-quarters full. Place the temporary aquarium in a bright area, but avoid direct sunlight. This will give the algae—the tadpoles' food—sufficient light for growth. Don't try to clean the pond water by straining out the tiny particles of dead and decaying plant material, because the tadpoles eat this material as well.

Details of Tadpole Development. A good way to continue your systematic observation of tadpoles is to record daily observations about their structure and behavior in a journal and sketch the tadpoles in different phases of life.

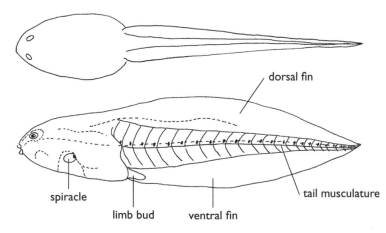

The dotted lines indicate the location of lateral line sense organ on this typical tadpole.

Write a description of a tadpole. What is it doing? With the help of a hand lens, you can discover how a newly hatched tadpole hangs on to plants. What is happening to the tail? Look for the feathery external gills on either side of the tadpole. How do you think it breathes? When do the external gills disappear? When do the hind legs appear? Does the tadpole seem to be gulping air at the water's surface? What is a possible explanation for this behavior? Did your tadpole stop eating? What might be happening?

If you have several tadpoles in a large aquarium, do they stay together (as in a school), or do they swim and eat singly? Do they tend to stay hidden in vegetation? Describe their camouflage. (See Chapter Note 7.)

TADPOLES

Species	Tadpole to Frog	Adult Lifespan
American toad	35–70 days	5–10 years
common toad	40–60 days	5 years plus
eastern spadefoot	48–63 days for early broods 16–20 days for late broods	5 years plus
wood frog	1–70 days	3 years plus
green frog	1–2 years	5 years plus
northern leopard frog	63–84 days	3 years plus
bullfrog	4 months–2 years	6 years plus
gray tree frog	50–60 days	Unknown
spring peeper	45–60 days	3 years plus

Frogs in a Terrarium. Frogs can be kept in a terrarium for a short period of time without suffering harm, but because toads are less dependent on water, you may want to use them instead. When you are handling a frog be sure your hands are wet, because hot, dry hands can harm the frog's delicate skin.

You can use a ten-gallon or larger aquarium for adult frogs. Put a rectangular plastic food-storage container into the aquarium and fill it with pond water. A two-cup size will work well. To supply the frog with fresh water, simply remove the container, clean it, and fill it with water.

Into the remaining space put some gravel and cover it with potting soil. Add woodland litter such as a few rocks, some moss, pieces of bark, small branches, and twigs. Finish your temporary frog habitat by placing a piece of screening over the top of the tank to prevent the frog from leaping out.

To feed your frog, you must supply it with live, active insects. A frog will not eat anything that does not move, no matter how hungry it may be. If you give it flying, wiggling insects such as crickets, flies, moths, caterpillars, slugs, snails, and worms, the frog will eat.

While you are holding the frog captive, make some additional observations about its structure and its behavior. For example, does the frog keep its eyes open when it eats? How does it sit? Write a description of a sitting frog. How many vocal sacs does it have? Where are they located?

When you finish your observations, be sure to return the frog to where you found it.

Effects of Temperature on Frog Calls. Herpetologists have learned that air temperature determines when frogs will call as well as the rate at which the calls are made. In the northern cricket frog (*Acris crepitans*), the call rate increases as the temperature increases. Similar results were noted in the advertisement call of the gray tree frog (*Hyla versicolor*) and in the release calls of several species of toads (*Bufo* spp.).

The chart below gives the range of air temperature at which certain frogs will call. Within this range the rate of the calls will change. The frog populations represented live in Louisiana, Georgia, Alabama, and Mississippi. How does the air temperature affect the rate of calling of frogs in your area?

Frogs are known to be sensitive to footfalls on the soil. They can quiet a

FROG CALLS

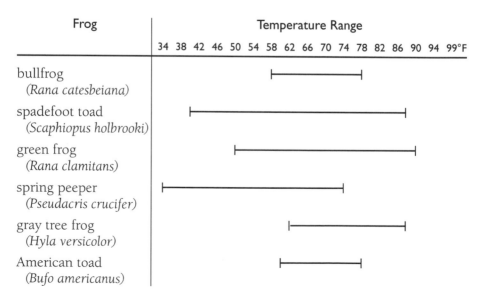

calling male many yards away. Try to sneak up on a calling frog. How close can you get to it before it stops calling?

Unsolved Mysteries. Although herpetologists have learned a great deal about frogs, there are still many mysteries to be solved. For example, how far do frogs travel from their winter shelters to reach their breeding pools? Do individual frogs go to the same pool each year to breed? Is this the same pool where they were hatched? How do the males identify the females of their species? Are frogs selective about where they lay their eggs? Where do they go and what do they do during the months that follow the breeding season? Perhaps you will have additional questions about frogs after you have spent some time observing them.

CHAPTER NOTES

1. Frog Calls. Calling is the most expensive activity in the life of an adult male frog in terms of the energy it requires. During the breeding season, male frogs call hundreds or thousands of times each night. The calling behavior of frogs can cost more than calories, as predators often use the calls to find tasty meals. The life of a frog is often the price a species pays for successful mating and the subsequent arrival of a new generation of frogs.

To produce calls, frogs take air into their lungs through their nostrils and pump the air rapidly back and forth from the lungs to a resonating chamber

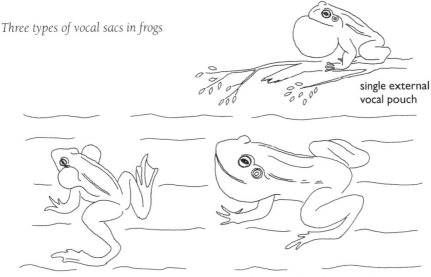

Three types of vocal sacs in frogs

single external vocal pouch

paired pouches, swelling into spheres above arm

single pouch, largely internal

called the vocal sac. In its journey the air passes over the vocal cords, causing them to vibrate and produce the familiar "croak." If you have ever tried to sleep near a frog pond, you know that croaking can continue throughout the night. When calling, a frog never needs to open its mouth.

2. Dip Nets. A good dip net has a long handle and a strong net bag with small mesh. The frame should be made of steel rather than aluminum, which is softer and tends to bend. You should be able to remove the frame so that you can replace torn bags as needed. Two suppliers: Carolina Biological Supply Co., Burlington, NC 27216; Wards Natural Science Establishment, Inc., PO Box 1712, Rochester, NY 14603.

3. Eyelids. Since frogs live both in water and on land, their eyes must be able to function both when exposed to air and when submerged. The biggest problem for an eye in open air is that it might dry up; to prevent this, frogs have thick eyelids. A thin, transparent fold called the nictitating membrane passes over the eye from bottom to top and serves to moisten and protect the eye by washing it with a thin film of tearlike liquid secreted by glands in the eye. This liquid contains lysozyme (an enzyme found in tears and in egg whites), which protects the eyes from bacteria, viruses, and fungi that sneak in under the eyelids.

Frogs cannot turn their heads as we do. To compensate for this lack of neck motion, frogs' bulging eyes provide them with a wide range of vision. This helps them find food and spot predators. You need only to sneak up on a frog to find out how well this design works. Frogs see well in twilight, and their night vision is extremely good. When frogs slip beneath the water's surface, the nictitating membrane rises to cover the eye. As tadpoles, their eyes are suited to life in the water. During this phase of their life, frogs' eyes more closely resemble those of fish than those of adult frogs.

4. Camouflage. Frogs have lightly colored underparts that contrast sharply with their darker tops. This is called countershading and is part of the frog's camouflage. The light coloring along the underside of the frog makes it difficult for a deep-swimming predator looking toward the surface of the water to see its prey as it swims along the surface. It is equally difficult to see the dark upper surface of the frog against the dark background of the pond bottom when looking down through the water.

The mottled pattern found on frogs also serves to make the frog difficult to see because the irregular outline breaks up the form of the frog's body. When looking for frogs, your eyes see the disruptive pattern as part of the vegetation in the frog's habitat.

5. Eye Shine. In the dark, our pupils become large black circles. Their

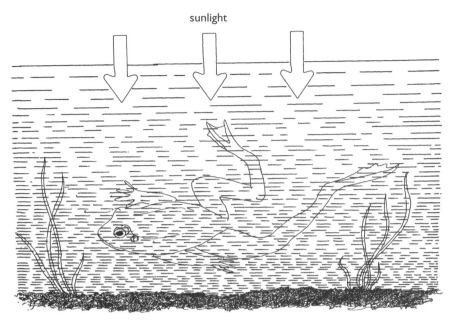

sunlight

Viewed through the water, the dark dorsal surface of the frog is difficult to see against the dark bottom of the pond.

size is controlled by the muscular irises, which contract as light diminishes. This process allows the maximum amount of available light to reach the rods of the retina; however, not all the light that passes through the pupil reaches the rods. Some of it is absorbed by surrounding tissues and is not available to illuminate our way in the dark.

Other critters have evolved different strategies for night vision. Owls, known for their nocturnal activity, have eyes that contain only rods, and their night vision is far superior to ours. The eyes of cats and waterbound dolphins contain many thousands more rods than our eyes do, and they see very well in the dark.

Another device developed by night-wandering animals is a layer of specialized cells called the *tapetum* that lies behind the retina. These mirrorlike cells reflect light back through the retina, where it has a second chance to stimulate vision cells. You can see the tapetum when the eyes of skunks, raccoons, cats, and other animals are caught in the beam of light from a flashlight or the headlight of a car. Look for the red, yellow, or green eye shine in our common night stalkers. You can learn to identify some animals by the color of their eye shine.

6. Frog Eggs. The bullfrog (*Rana catesbeiana*) produces an enormous egg mass, two to four feet across. Each of the several thousand eggs is contained in a gelatinous envelope. The green frog (*Rana clamitans*) deposits 1,000 to 3,000 eggs in a surface film. Each egg is enclosed in two jellylike envelopes. The egg mass may be attached to vegetation or free floating. A spring peeper (*Pseudacris crucifer*) individually deposits 250 to 1,000 very small (two-mm.) eggs, which are generally attached to vegetation. The 2,000 eggs of a gray tree frog (*Hyla versicolor*) are laid in packets of 6 to 45 eggs each that float freely or are attached to vegetation. The American toad (*Bufo americanus*) deposits 4,000 to 8,000 eggs in long, double strands. Eastern wood frogs (*Rana sylvatica*) produce a mass of 1,000-plus eggs attached to submerged twigs or resting free on the bottom of the pond. Fowlers toad (*B. fowleri*) lays up to 8,000 eggs in strands in aquatic vegetation. The northern leopard frog (*Rana pipiens*) deposits 4,000 to 6,500 eggs in masses in shallow water, sometimes attached to twigs.

7. Tadpole Development. A newly hatched tadpole lacks a mouth. In some species the tadpole attaches itself by means of a sucker under its head, which you can see with the aid of a hand lens.

Behind the tadpole's head there are a pair of feathery growths, which are external gills. The tadpoles use these gills to remove dissolved oxygen from the water. Through the process of diffusion, dissolved oxygen passes into the tadpole's bloodstream and waste products such as carbon dioxide are removed. Water escapes from the tadpole's body through a tiny hole called a spiracle.

The main food for the tadpole is pond scum, consisting of algae (small plants) and bacteria. Included in the diet is the decaying plant material from the bottom of the pond.

Soon the tadpole will lose its gills and develop a set of lungs. You will know that the tadpole has become an air-breathing creature when you see it swim to the surface of the water and gulp for air.

Tadpoles have a sensory perception system called the *lateral line system,* composed of sense organs that appear as a series of light and dark dots. The line of dots form curving rows on top of the head and around the eyes and sometimes extend to the tail, making three irregular rows on each side of the tadpole. This system is similar to the lateral line system found in fish and allows the tadpoles to detect low-frequency vibrations, turbulence, and pressure changes such as those made by passing creatures or by ardent tadpole collectors wading through the pond. Vibrations from the tadpoles' watery environment are channeled to sensory receptors on the lateral line system. It is believed that this system is responsible for keeping schools of tadpoles together.

CHAPTER 9

Turtles

TANTALIZING TURTLES

Finding a turtle is almost always a pleasant surprise. These slow-moving beasts plod doggedly through woodlands, meadows, and wetlands. From March to October, you might even stumble upon a turtle in your garden or navigating across your lawn. Finding them at the edge of a roadway stirs benevolent feelings and triggers protective behavior, as we hurry to remove them from danger.

Turtles are curious creatures. Their solitary nature has long intrigued and mystified us, but though they have been the subject of much interest and speculation, surprisingly little is known about how they make their living. Some species of turtles are known only by their appearance, leaving the mysteries about their biology yet to be discovered. Technologies such as radio-telemetry today are helping scientists gain new information.

Turtles, snakes, and other reptiles are grouped with amphibians in a branch of zoology called herpetology. The term is derived from the Greek word *herpeton,* which means "crawling things." Even though reptiles and amphibians are very different kinds of creatures, early naturalists thought the two groups of animals were more closely related than they really are. The practice of grouping them together has historical roots and persists today. There is some confusion over the terms tortoise, terrapin, and turtle. Tortoises are essentially creatures of the land, while terrapins live in the water. The term *turtle* is generally appropriate for all.

Turtles have been around for a long time. The armored bodies we see today have remained unchanged for about 200 million years. Turtles were present when the dinosaurs first developed, and they witnessed the cataclysmic events that caused the mass extinction of those great reptiles. Many turtle species were also lost, but others endured, and the turtles we see today are descendants of those survivors.

Much remains unknown about the origin of turtles. Scientists believe that their forebears may date as far back as 250 million years ago, to a primitive two-foot-long reptile. This ancestor carried a row of unfused bony plates over its back and tail. The plates eventually fused and spread out over the body to form a primitive, tubelike shell. This armor protected the animal from predators, as well as from extremes in temperature, but did not interfere with its stout walking legs. Over time, there were further changes in the reptilian ancestor, until it eventually looked much like the turtle we know today. Those early but fully formed turtles differed somewhat from those we see today, however. They were unable to pull their heads into the neck fold of skin, and they

Ankylosaurus lived in the Cretaceous period and resembled a very large turtle, but its bony plates and spines were unfused.

had tiny teeth, but they did possess a shell, the unmistakable hallmark of the turtle. Across eons of time, this basic characteristic has remained unchanged.

The new blueprint of the turtle's shell shows several modifications in the animal's body plan. Unlike the shell of the ancestral turtles, the bony upper shell, or carapace, is firmly attached to the flattened ribs that support it. The bony portion of the shell is now covered by close-fitting horny sections called scutes, which vary in color and design and aid in identifying different species of turtles. Like the rafters in the roof of a house, the pitch of the ribs determine the shape of the carapace; some turtle shells are dome shaped, while others are relatively flat.

Proganochelys, extinct for more than 200 million years, resembled a modern turtle.

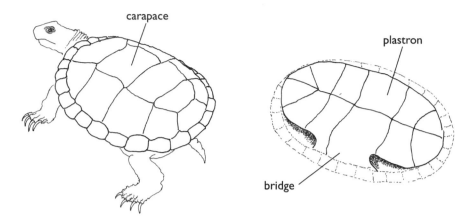

Turtles have an upper shell, or carapace, and a lower shell, or plastron, connected by a bony bridge.

The carapace and plastron are made of bony plates, or scutes, that fit closely together. The scutes are covered with a horny material that resembles our fingernails. This outer layer is sometimes shed or worn off, but as the turtle grows in size, it cannot shed its shell to accommodate the increasing size of the bones and other organs that underlie it. Instead, new material grows beneath the older horny material and covers the constantly enlarging

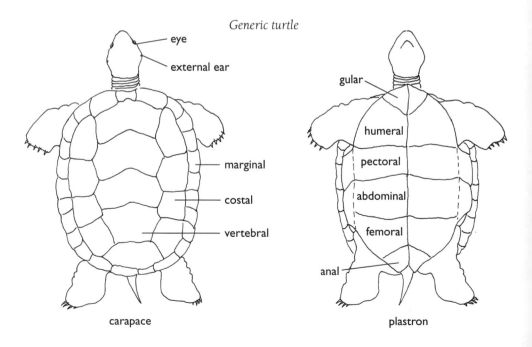

THE PLAYERS

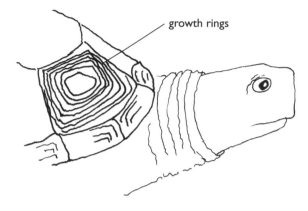

growth rings

bone of the shell. The new growth extends beyond the old shield and produces a ring around its edges. Like the concentric rings found in tree trunks, each ring on a shield represents a year of growth. Because the rings are easier to see on young turtles, the technique is most accurately used on turtles up to about the age of eight. In warm climates, growth continues throughout the year, so it is difficult to determine the age of the turtles.

The development of the shell required additional modifications in turtle design. Turtles have lungs, but since the ribs are fused to the ridged shell, chest muscles like ours would not help them inhale and exhale air. Instead, they have three sets of special muscles that control their lungs. Two muscles, one on each side of the body, increase the size of the body cavity. This activity pulls air into the lungs. The air is forced out of the lungs by a third muscle pushing against the internal organs. When you observe a turtle, it may seem that muscles in the animal's throat are involved in the breathing process, but the movement actually is a result of breathing, not the cause of it. Some turtles can survive without air for an amazing six months.

Turtles are toothless. Their jaws are covered with a horny material that forms a beak, which is a fine tool for tearing animal and plant material into bite-size pieces. If you watch turtles in captivity eat raw meat, you will see that this arrangement works well for them, and the absence of teeth is not a handicap.

What turtles eat depends primarily on where they live. Those that spend most of their time on land are generally herbivores, tending to eat only plant material. Some aquatic turtles feed on the plants or animals they find in the ponds and quiet streams where they live. Some dine on carrion, and others eat only small animals. Because turtles are slow moving and cannot chase their prey, they use a hide-and-pounce technique, which seems to work well for them. Snapping turtles have been known to grab unsuspecting ducks by their legs, drag them underwater, and make a meal of their captives.

A turtle's skin is scaly and tough, helping prevent injury from attacks by predators or abrasion from rocks or other obstacles in the environment. There is a thin surface layer of cells that flakes off from time to time. This doesn't cause the turtle's color to change, however, because the cells that give the turtle its color lie deeper in the skin.

Most turtles mate in the spring, although some wait until summer, and a few even until autumn to perform this annual ritual. From early spring into autumn, you might see turtles crawling resolutely through woodlands, making their way along roadside ditches, or slogging through the muddy realm of ponds and swamps. When it comes to egg laying, turtles are not bound to fresh water or damp places, as are frogs and other amphibians. All turtles lay their eggs on land, even those that live in the water for the rest of the year. After mating, a female generally travels several hundred feet from the water in search of a suitable place to build a nest. When she finds the right spot, she will begin to dig a hole with her sharp-toed front feet. After excavating the surface layer of earth, which has been softened by spring rains, she will put her hind legs to work. Aided by sharp claws, a characteristic shared by all reptiles that have feet, she will laboriously dig a deeper inner hole that will cradle her eggs. When the hole is sufficiently deep, she deposits her eggs into it, covers the hole with excavated dirt, and ambles away. Large turtles have been known to deposit as many as fifty-two eggs in the nest, at a rate of two to three a minute.

Turtles have amniotic eggs, in which the developing young float in a liquid and receive nourishment from the yolk. You can see these same essentials by carefully opening and examining the white and yolk of a chicken egg. Everything required by the developing turtle is present in the egg, which is protected from damage by a leathery shell—a covering that resists damage far better than the brittle shell of a chicken egg. Turtle eggs are about one inch in diameter and vary little from one species to another. They are usually white, but you may find turtle eggs with a faint tint of pink or blue.

The female doesn't incubate the eggs, and the warmth for incubation comes from the earth. The eggs may take two or more months to hatch, but if cold weather arrives before the young emerge, the developmental process enters a period of dormancy, and hatching does not occur until the spring.

When the young turtles hatch from the protection of their eggs, they are vulnerable to attack by raccoons, skunks, snakes, birds, and other hungry predators. The hatchlings receive neither food nor shelter from their mother. They will grow old and die without ever knowing her.

Nesting spotted turtle. Eggs emerge from the cloacal opening.

In some species, the sex of the offspring is determined by temperature. If the eggs are incubated at about 78 degrees F. (25 degrees C.), males will emerge, but if incubation occurs at 86 degrees F. (31 degrees C.) or higher, the hatchlings will be females. Several external variables are responsible for these potential temperature differences. The eggs are buried at random depths. As the female tries to replace the earth removed to make the nest hole, she scratches the earth with her hind claws, causing some eggs to be blanketed with more soil than others. The result is that the eggs in the nest will not be uniformly insulated and warmed. Weather also plays a part in determining the incubation temperature of the eggs in the nest. These influences of external forces on the developing embryos guarantee that both male and female hatchlings will emerge, but there is no way to predict the ratio of male to female hatchlings in the wild.

In all animals, heat production and regulation of internal temperature are essential for metabolic activity to take place. In birds and mammals, the source of body heat and the mechanism for control of that heat are internal, and the temperatures produced are stable within a given range. These ani-

Hatching turtles are at greatest risk from predators as they first emerge from their nests.

mals are referred to as endotherms. In turtles, the body heat produced is conducted to the outside environment faster than they can replace it. Thus, the turtle's internal body temperature is controlled mostly by external factors, such as the daily fluctuations of temperature and seasonal variations. Turtles and other animals that function this way are called ectotherms. (The terms "cold-blooded" and "warm-blooded" are old-fashioned and have fallen into disuse, since they do not provide a realistic idea of the metabolic differences between these two groups of animals.)

As the ambient temperature falls, turtles cannot generate enough body heat to maintain a constant internal temperature. Without a sufficiently high internal temperature, turtles cannot keep their vital processes, such as circulation, respiration, and digestion, working effectively. By the end of August, shorter days and cooler nights herald the coming of autumn. The turtles instinctively know that these events signal a cooling trend that leads to frigid winds and icy landscapes. They know that it's time to prepare now for the cold season. As the temperature drops, turtles become increasingly inactive. When the temperature is about 50 degrees F., turtles will seek protection beneath piles of leaf litter. But when the temperature drops below freezing, many species, including painted, musk, and snapping turtles, return to the ponds that fed them during warmer weather and crawl beneath blankets of mud. While beneath the mud in a state of suspended animation, a turtle's internal functions are slowed considerably. A painted turtle, for example, reduces its heartbeat to a mere one beat in ten minutes. In the reduced metabolic state brought on by the cold, turtles can go without food and air for a very long time.

Different turtle species have various ways of surviving the cold weather. Painted turtles that hatch from their eggs in early autumn remain throughout the winter about four inches below their earthen cover. They will surface sometime in May, after the spring sun has warmed the air. The eastern box turtle digs a den about three to four feet into the soil and remains there tightly closed inside its "box."

During winter's milder days, turtles are often seen sunning themselves on fallen logs, rocks, clumps of dead grass, and rafts of sphagnum moss, where

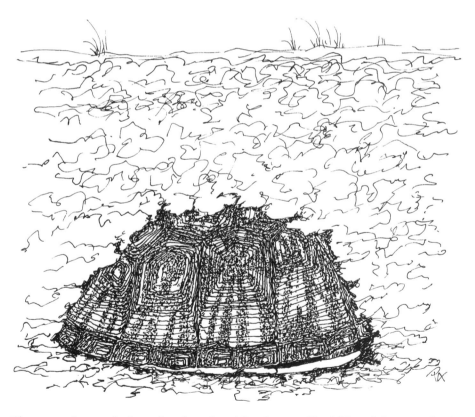

The eastern box turtle digs a den about 3 to 4 feet down and backfills with leaves and soil to cover itself. Snug in its shell, it is protected from the winter's chilling cold.

they may pile up two or three deep. You can observe turtles basking even in the winter on warm days.

Habitat destruction is a major threat to the welfare of turtles. Their habitats are being converted at an alarming rate into shopping malls, housing developments, and parking lots. The continued agricultural use of insecticides and pesticides is responsible for further damage to those places that turtles call home. Several species are currently on the protected list.

In the activities that follow, you will have a chance to learn more about specific turtles that you are likely to find during the spring. Under most circumstances, you do not need to remove turtles from their habitat. Before you do remove a turtle from its habitat, find out which turtles are on the protected list in your state. It is generally all right to keep a turtle outdoors in a pen with food and water for a short period of time while you make your observations. When you release the turtle, put it back where you found it, as long as that place is not in the middle of a road. If you found the turtle in a potentially dangerous situation, put it in a safe place but heading in the same direction it was going when you found it. Turtles found in the spring or early summer are generally females looking for a good nesting spot.

THE WORLD OF TURTLES

What you will need

basic kit
stopwatch
tape measure
patience

Science skills

observing
recording
inferring

OBSERVATIONS

Some of the activities presented here will require you to get close to water or wade into a pond. *Do not do any of these activities alone.* Wear waterproof clothing, boots, and where the depth is uncertain, a Coast Guard–approved life jacket. Use your field journal to describe what you see, and record any questions you have so you can explore them at another time.

Turtle Types

Wood and Pond Turtles. These turtles are adapted for living both on land and in the water. Their legs are strong enough for walking on land, and they have webbed toes that make them effective swimmers. Their cumbersome shells do not interfere with their ability to swim. They are omnivores, eating both plant and animal material.

Land Tortoises. These turtles have heavy, bulky shells and move more slowly than wood and pond turtles. Their front legs are adapted for shoveling soil and sand aside. The front edge of the bottom shell is curved upward so that it doesn't get hung up on obstacles but instead helps the turtles slide up and over obstacles, like the upcurved front of a sled. With their heavy armor, they don't need to run from predators, and this, combined with their diet of plant materials, makes life in the slow lane possible.

Soft-shelled Turtles. These turtles seldom leave their watery world, where they live partly buried in the mud. The soft-shelled turtle has a thin, leathery shell that resembles a pancake and a flat body adapted to wiggling into the mud for protection, leaving only the head projecting. This turtle is colored to look like mud or muddy stones.

Turtle Anatomy. The ideal way to observe a wild creature is to avoid anything that interferes with it or disturbs its normal routine. When you are observing turtles, be very careful to do no harm, both to the creature and to its habitat. Some turtles, like the box turtle, withdraw into their shells if you pick them up, but others have long, agile necks and may reach back to bite you, so be careful both for your sake and for the turtle's.

Since many turtle species tend to retract their legs, head, and tail when picked up, this is a good time to look at the suit of armor it wears. The top shell, or carapace, derived from the Spanish word for "shield," adheres to the turtle's backbone and ribs. In many turtles, this shell has a dome shape. The steepness of the dome varies and is dependent on the curve of the turtle's ribs that lie beneath it. In some species, the carapace is almost flat. In others, it is high and boxy. The bottom shell, which adheres to the breastbone, is called the plastron, from the Italian word for "breastplate," a piece of armor that soldiers strapped across the chest to deflect arrows and blows from swords. How do the carapace and plastron compare in size, shape, and color?

Turn the turtle on its back and examine where the top and bottom shell are joined. Where are they joined together? Is there a hinge? Is this bridge rigid? Box turtles' shells are joined by a hinge that permits the complete or partial closing of the shell when the turtle pulls in its limbs and head. The hinges are designed so that the turtle may close up from underneath. Make a drawing of the upper and lower shells.

The diagrams of the box turtle and the snapping turtle illustrate two extremes in plastron design. The crosslike shape of the snapping turtle's lower shell allows greater freedom of movement, but protection of limbs, head, and neck from below has been sacrificed. The snapping turtle's head, neck, and limbs are extremely agile, and it can be dangerous unless you are very careful

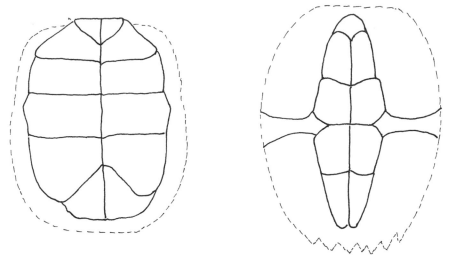

Plastron of box turtle
(not to scale)

Plastron of snapping turtle
(not to scale)

and know how to handle it. In contrast, the box turtle has given up agility for complete protection from its shell.

People often think they see a snake in a pond, only to find out they were looking at the head and neck of a turtle. How long is the neck of your captive? Write a description of what happens when it withdraws its head into its neck. Can you see why a sweater is described as having a "turtleneck"? What is the shape of the turtle's head? Do you see any color or pattern?

Describe the turtle's mouth. Do you see any teeth? How do you think the turtle eats fish, worms, snails, or pieces of meat? Would "beak" be a good description for this type of mouth?

What color are the eyes? If you see color, where is it located? Is it part of the eye, or is it around the eye? When the turtle blinks, look for the third eyelids, or nictitating membranes. These are translucent folds under the turtle's eyelids that protect the eyes. If an eye is touched by dust particles or other debris, the membrane vertically slides across the eye, washing the eye with tears as it moves. Do these membranes move with the eyelids, or do they move independently? Do the nictitating membranes move up and down like the eyelids, or do they move from the outside of the eye to the inside, toward the turtle's nose?

Examine the turtle's legs. Rub your finger along the exposed limbs. How do they feel? How many claws are on the front feet? On the back feet? Are the

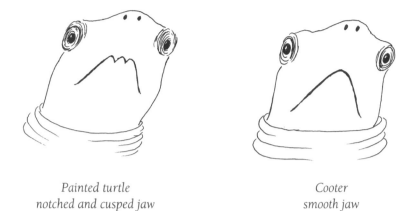

Painted turtle
notched and cusped jaw

Cooter
smooth jaw

toes webbed? Is the webbing on the front or hind feet? What is an explanation for this? Watch the turtle swim. Does it use its hind feet and front feet in the same way? Which feet are the paddles?

Watch your turtle walk. How much of its body is visible? Is its neck fully extended? What does it do with its head? What does it do with its tail?

Describe the location and appearance of the legs, tail, and head when a turtle is in its shell. How much of these parts remain visible? Can you see the turtle's eyes or nose? Is there anything soft for a predator to bite?

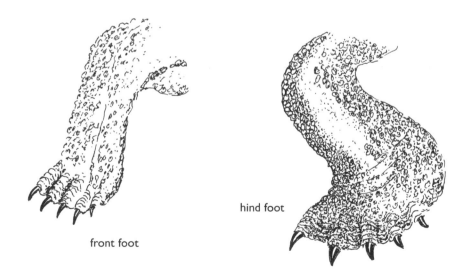

front foot

hind foot

The webbing on the turtle's hind feet is more highly developed.

Turtle Identification. The outline and illustrations below include some of our more common turtles and will help you identify the turtles you find.

1. Spotted turtle *(Clemmys guttata)*

    Habitat. Shallow ponds, marshes, small woodland streams, and rain-filled pools in wooded areas, along dirt roads, and in rain-soaked pastures.

    Field marks. The blue-black to black top shell is smooth and low. It's handsomely decorated with randomly placed lemon yellow spots. The polkadot pattern differs for each individual. Head and limbs are similarly spotted but are gray to black. The dark pigment melanin increases with age, so the top shells of older turtles are frequently spotless. The underside edges of the upper shell are marked with yellow. The female has a yellow chin and orange eyes; the male has a tan chin and brown eyes. The male's tail is almost twice as long as the female's tail, and the male's carapace grows to about five inches.

    Behavior. Look for spotted turtles during the daylight hours, when they sun themselves on floating logs, rocks, or clumps of grasses and reeds near water's edge. They may bask in the company of painted turtles. You may see them hunting for food as well. These turtles don't engage in aimless wandering. With darkness, they burrow under vegetation, into muddy bottoms of wetlands, where they remain until dawn.

    Food preferences. Feed on grasses and green algae underwater. Also eat live or dead aquatic insect larvae, small crustaceans, snails, and tadpoles.

    Predators. Bald eagles, skunks, and raccoons.

    Breeding and nesting. Early March, when water temperatures reach 46 degrees F. and the air reaches 54 degrees F. Dry, sandy fields and the margins of hayfields are choice nest spots. Vegetation such as bluestem grasses or sweet ferns generally shelters a nest.

    Other remarks. Spotted turtles have keen senses of smell and sight. These turtles may live into their twenties.

2. Painted turtle *(Chrysemys picta)*

    *Habitat.*Permanent shallow waters with muddy bottoms and plenty of vegetation, such as partially overgrown ponds.

    Field marks. A handsome small turtle with a flat top shell that is olive with yellow or red markings along its edge. The carapace colors blend with the patterns and colors of shade, plants, and earth, camouflaging the turtle, but you may see the scarlet rim of the shells when it dips beneath the surface of the pond. The plates on the upper shell sides are bordered with yellow. The lower shell is bright yellow-

Range of the spotted turtle

Spotted turtle (Clemmys guttata), *3½ to 5 inches*

orange. The head and neck are adorned with yellow streaks behind the eye. Yellow stripes of uniform length become red as they extend to throat. Limbs and tail are also speckled and streaked with red. There are four subspecies of the painted turtle, each of which sports its own characteristic pattern of red and yellow. Adults measure six to eight inches in length.

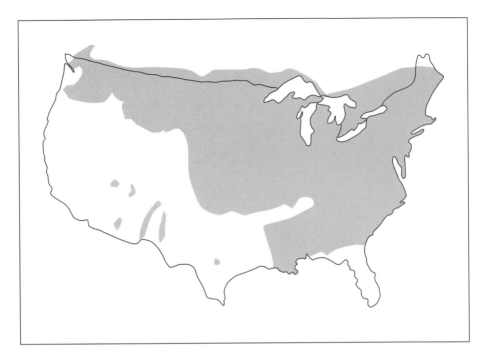

Range of the painted turtle

Painted turtle (Chrysemys picta), 6 to 8 inches

Behavior. In the northern part of their range, look for them from March into November. They often are seen basking on logs, rocks, and amid clumps of floating grasses early in the morning and again in the afternoon. You may also be able to see these turtles swimming beneath winter ice. Farther south, they emerge sooner and begin hibernation later. Be careful if you want to observe them for details; the slightest movement may send them spilling into the water and out of sight. At night they sleep on the muddy sheets that line their ponds. They don't ever stray far from their watery homes.

Food preferences. Animal or plant material of any type, living or dead, including earthworms, leeches, slugs, snails, crayfish, spiders, water striders, beetles, dragonflies, springtails, damselflies, and dead fish. Forage in the morning and late in the afternoon, along the bottom of ponds and among algae. Eat underwater and seem unable to swallow their food if out of water.

Predators. Primarily raccoons, but chipmunks, skunks, badgers, foxes, garter snakes, fish crows, and humans also destroy nests.

Breeding and nesting. Nests may be found along the tree-lined margins of fields, a few feet to several yards away from the tree line, along roadsides, and in gravel pits. Only females leave the pond, and they do so when ready to lay their eggs.

Other remarks. One of the most numerous turtles in North America. One reason for its success is that it is able to live in ponds close to our homes in the suburbs and in cities. May live some twenty years.

3. Eastern box turtle (*Terrapene carolina*)

Habitat. Primarily woodland turtles, you may find them in neglected pastureland and marshy meadows. Although considered a land turtle, they will take to water. They will soak in mud for hours to wash away the dust and to escape hot summer air.

Field marks. Unique hinged lower shell that can be closed tightly by strong muscles against the upper shell, protecting the turtle against all predators. The seal is so tight that even a thin knife blade cannot be wedged between the shells when they are closed. Easily recognized high, domed, brownish top shell with yellow or orange rays, and spots or bars in each plate. Tan to brown lower shell that may or may not be patterned. Black to reddish skin streaked or spotted with red, yellow, or orange. There are four subspecies that differ somewhat in color. Males can be distinguished from females by eye color—red

Range of the eastern box turtle

Eastern box turtle (Terrapene carolina), *4 to 6 inches*

THE PLAYERS

or pink in males, and generally brown, but sometimes purple or gray, in females. Adults measure four to six inches in length.

Behavior. From April through October, you may find them sunning themselves at the edges of fields or roads or in forest groves. They avoid the heat of the day by hiding under logs, in clumps of decaying leaves, vacant mammal burrows, or holes they dig into the mud. Box turtles have fairly well-defined home territories that are usually less than 750 square feet, which they wander freely. Because they have a strong sense of direction, they seldom get lost.

Food preferences. Forage on land or in shallow water. The young are carnivorous, but as they grow older, box turtles prefer a more vegetarian diet, including mushrooms, blueberries, elderberries, wild grapes, strawberries, tomatoes, mayapples, wintergreen, and mosses. Blackberries are their favorite food, and box turtles have been known to gorge on them. Animal foods include insects, snails, slugs, earthworms, and spiders.

Predators. Badgers, foxes, skunks, barn owls, crows, and snakes destroy many nests and feed on young. Adults are often attacked by carnivores such as raccoons, skunks, coyotes, and dogs. Box turtles found with mutilated legs are usually victims of such attacks.

Breeding and nesting. Nests may be found in sandy fields and meadows, cultivated gardens, along roadsides, and in ditches. The female digs a flask-shaped nest in three to five hours, lays up to eight elliptical eggs, and covers them with the excavated dirt.

Other remarks. Can live more than 120 years and are the longest-lived vertebrates in North America.

4. Snapping turtle (*Chelydra serpentina*)

Habitat. Almost every kind of shallow freshwater habitat, especially slow-moving streams with soft, muddy bottoms. Although these are water turtles, you have a good chance of finding one on land, and during the early spring, you might see one roaming through a roadside ditch, along a streambank, or in a salt marsh.

Field marks. A snapping turtle looks like a prehistoric animal that wandered into present geologic time. It has a large, pointed head and a strong beak that is excellent for tearing meat. Its tail is as long as or longer than the carapace and has three rows of bumps down its length. The huge, bumpy top shell is brown or deep gray to black, providing camouflage, and each plate is generally patterned with radi-

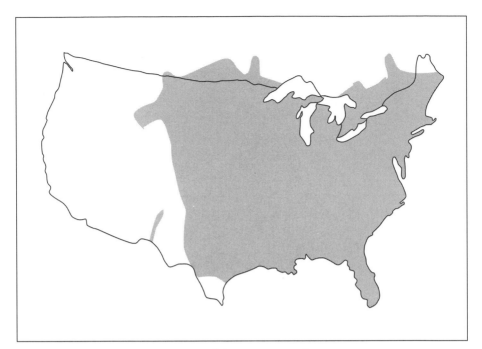

Range of the snapping turtle

Snapping turtle (Chelydra serpentina), *18 to 32 inches*

ating lines. The rear of the top shell is notched. The cross-shaped bottom shell is much smaller than the top shell and does not protect an overturned turtle. Webbed toes and heavy claws indicate a good swimmer and efficient digger. The snapper's design is fitting for the life of a bottom dweller. Snappers generally weigh twenty-five to thirty pounds, although adults can reach forty pounds and a length of three feet.

Behavior. The snapper spends most of its time on the bottom of a pond or buried in the mud, with only its eyes and the tip of its nose visible. It must extend its neck to raise its nostrils above the water from time to time to breathe. The snapper may also hide in tangles of roots and under tree stumps. It can anchor itself to an object by wrapping its strong tail around it. A swift walker, it can also lunge and jump. The snapping turtle can move its head with surprising speed, and its sharp beak tears very well—a compensation for the loss of protection from its abbreviated shells. It is aggressive on land but docile in the water.

Food preferences. Plants and animals, including salamanders, small turtles, frogs, snakes, and birds. Forages along weedy and muddy bottoms, where it eats almost anything its powerful hooked jaws can rip into bite-size pieces.

Predators. Hognose snakes, mink, crows, bears, foxes, wolves, and raccoons eat snapper eggs. Hatchlings and young turtles provide food for herons, egrets, bitterns, shrikes, large hawks, bald eagles, bullfrogs, and water snakes.

Breeding and nesting. Nests are dug in loose, sandy soil or loam along railroads, roadside ditches, and beaches. Sometimes make their nests in beaver lodges. Females lay their eggs at night.

Other remarks. Do not treat these fast-moving turtles casually. When handled improperly, they can inflict serious wounds. It is best to leave them alone.

5. Wood turtle (Clemmys insculpta)

Habitat. The wood turtle wanders far from water in late spring and summer, when you may find them lumbering through pastures and woodlands. In early spring and in the autumn, the turtles prefer the wetter environs of swamps, brooks, and ponds, because they spend the winter in the muddy bottoms of these damp places.

Field marks. The roughly sculptured concentric ridges on the plates of the gray-brown carapace make this turtle easy to identify. Head and feet

Range of the wood turtle

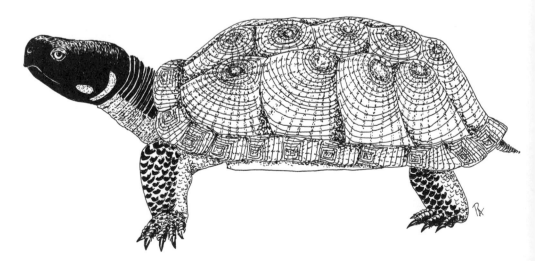

Wood turtle (Clemmys insculpta), 5½ to 7½ inches

are rusty brown to black, and the limbs, neck, and tail are a muted brick red—ideal for camouflaging the turtle among dead leaves and grasses. The carapace of the adult wood turtle measures about six and one-half inches.

Behavior. Active during daylight from April to November. In spring and summer, these turtles travel far from water to pastures, woodlands, and upland fields. They are good swimmers. Like other turtles, wood turtles bask, but they usually engage in the activity individually; rarely will you find more than one wood turtle basking together. When cold weather comes, they hibernate in muskrat burrows, snuggling beneath the banks of streams and ponds, although they have been seen swimming under the ice during the winter.

Food preferences. When on land, eat the same fare as ground-nesting birds, including strawberries, blackberries, and leaves of various wildflowers, but seem to prefer mushrooms. In water, eat aquatic insects and animals.

Predators. Raccoons, rodents, and striped skunks eat wood turtle eggs. Feral cats, dogs, and opossums feed on young wood turtles.

Breeding and nesting. The nesting season is from May to July. Well-drained, moist sand or soil provides good nest material. Female digs a hollow in fields, along sunny roadsides, or in gravelly ditches, where she deposits about twelve eggs.

6. Musk turtle (*Sternotherus odoratus*)

Habitat. Shallow ponds with clear water. Spends an inactive winter at the bottom of a pond or in a muskrat den. Comes on land only to lay eggs. In general, keeps a low profile.

Field marks. Highly arched, smooth, brown carapace provides good camouflage for a turtle that spends a great deal of time on muddy pond bottoms. The carapace is frequently covered with algae, which makes it difficult to distinguish the turtle from rocks or chunks of wood on the muddy bottom. Two yellow lines, one above and one below the eye, extend along each side of the head and neck. Mature musk turtles measure about four to five inches in length.

Behavior. Most active after sunset. Live and feed on the bottoms of ponds, reservoirs, lakes, and slow-running streams. Musk turtles snap, and with their strong beaks, they can inflict a serious wound.

Food preferences. Small fish, worms, insects, and tadpoles.

Predators. Raccoons, foxes, and skunks eat the eggs. Snakes, frogs, herons, and fish feed on hatchlings.

Range of the musk turtle

Musk turtle (Sternotherus odoratus), *4 to 5 inches*

THE PLAYERS

Breeding and nesting. Visit land in late June only to lay their eggs. Egg laying in May and June seems to be a haphazard affair. The females deposit their eggs in shallow nests on the surface of the ground, in leaf litter, tucked into rotting logs, or in muskrat lodges.

Other remarks. The musk turtle is nicknamed stinkpot, for the odor that is secreted from musk glands near the base of the limbs.

Behavior. While it is fun to be able to identify the kinds of turtles you find, it is even more interesting to watch their behavior. Try to answer the following questions about each turtle you find: What does it eat? How does it catch its prey? Is it a carnivore or an herbivore? How does it avoid its enemies? How does it defend itself? How does it adjust to seasonal changes? How does it raise a family?

Basking. Many humans go to the beach to lie in the sun. Turtles also engage in basking, but they do it to raise their body temperature. Basking time can range from a few minutes to several hours. If possible, observe several turtles from the time when they begin to bask until they cease the activity. How long does each kind of turtle bask? Enlist your friends to observe basking behavior. How do your observations compare?

How many basking turtles are there? Are they all the same kind of turtle? Often two or three turtles stack themselves on each other. This is called "piling." Scientists are not sure why turtles engage in this activity, because only the top turtle in the pile receives beneficial heating from the sun. It does not seem to be related to a shortage of space, nor does it seem to be a strategy for

An important part of the day for many turtles is the time spent basking in the sun.

avoiding predators, because the top turtles often scramble into the water at a slight disturbance while the bottom turtle remains. Explore this by seeing how close you can get to them before they slide off their perch and disappear into the water. Do any remain on the perch?

On what are your turtles basking? Is it a log, a rock, or sphagnum moss? Turtles prefer sphagnum moss because it is a good conductor of heat. Rocks seem to be their second choice, and logs rank third.

EXPLORATIONS

Fright Response. Where are the eyes placed on a turtle's head? Are they in the front of the head like our eyes or on the side of the head like a bird's? What is the advantage to the turtle in having its eyes placed where they are? How close can you get to the turtle before it withdraws into its shell? Can you get closer to the turtle by approaching it from a different direction? Which approach can you use to get the closest before the turtle tucks itself into the safety of its shell?

How much of the turtle can you see when it withdraws? Pick up the turtle when it has pulled itself into its shell. (*Do not* pick up a snapping turtle.) Can you see more of it from the underside than from the top?

Based on these observations, write an explanation of why you think the turtle has been able to survive over millions of years.

Speed. Some turtles move much faster than others. Stage a turtle race with some of your friends and their turtles. Most turtles you might find would be suitable, but *do not use snapping turtles,* which will bite if not handled properly.

To set up your racetrack, make a circle six feet in diameter. Then make another circle around the first with a diameter of twelve feet. In the center of the first circle, place a bull's-eye. This will be the starting place for the race, so be sure it is large enough to accommodate all the competing turtles.

You will need a timekeeper with a stopwatch, whose job it will be to call the start of the race and who will call the end when the first turtle crosses over the outside circle.

Predict which turtle will move the fastest and which the slowest. On what did you base your predictions? The turtles' overall size? The way the plastrons fit the limbs? Do the legs seem to have much freedom of movement, or does the lower shell fit snugly around the turtle's legs?

When you have made your predictions, put the turtles on the bull's-eye and let the race begin. The winner always gets a ribbon, and why not present the last turtle to finish with a special prize for slowness?

If no one else in the neighborhood has a turtle, you can still have a race in which your turtle competes against itself. It can challenge its own records. With the help of a stopwatch and a tape measure, you can find out how fast your turtle moves.

Trial #	Distance	Time
1		
2		
3		

Sense of Smell. To find out if turtles can smell, try a little investigation. Hang two bags, one containing some chopped meat and another filled with sand, in a box with your turtle. Which of the two bags attracts the meat-eating turtle? Repeat the investigation on several different occasions, hanging the bags in different locations in the turtle box. What happens each time? Does the turtle peck at the bag containing the meat while ignoring the bag containing the sand? What generalizations can you make about turtles and their ability to smell, based on their behavior?

Temperature and Turtle Activity. The internal temperature and the metabolic rate of turtles and other reptiles are controlled by the temperature of the air around them. The colder the air becomes, the less active the turtles will be. During the early spring, visit a local pond and measure the temperature of the air and that of the water near the surface and at the bottom of the pond (attach a thermometer to a stick long enough to reach the bottom of the pond). Record the readings. Return to your pond regularly as the temperature increases through April. On what date do you see your first turtle? What was the temperature of the pond and of the air that day?

Turtle Overturn. Occasionally a turtle will need to climb over a log or some other obstacle in its path, or it may tumble down a sandy bank or a pile of rocks. When this happens, the turtle may flip over and land upside down. This is a potentially dangerous situation for the turtle. Lying upside down in the sun can be fatal if the turtle cannot right itself quickly.

How does the turtle right itself? To find out, gently put your turtle on its back and watch its behavior. Does it use its head or legs in the process? How does the turtle shell help or hinder this process? In your notebook, record what the turtle does with its head, neck, tail, and legs. How long does it take the turtle to turn itself right side up? Most can right themselves after a few tries. What kinds of turtles do you think have the most difficulty turning themselves right side up? Do you think the length of the legs might be a factor? What part does the design of the shell play?

CHAPTER 10

Beavers, Muskrats, and Raccoons

MAMMALS OF WET PLACES

Like most mammals that live in the wild, beavers are active at night, when they are less likely to be spotted by predators. Their preference for working in the diminishing evening light means that most people have not had an opportunity to observe them building their dams and lodges. Although we have come to know beavers through folklore and legend, most of us have not seen them in the wild. Beavers (*Castor canandensis*) belong to a subgroup of mammals called rodents or Rodentia, from the Latin for "to gnaw," along with muskrats, minks, and river otters.

Today's beaver is a descendant of a very big rodent, also a builder, that lived about a million years ago. Fossil evidence shows that these rodents weighed about seven hundred pounds and measured about eight feet tall when sitting on their haunches. They lived in the swamps and marshes before and during the most recent ice age, which ended about ten thousand years ago. During this cold period, which affected one-third of the earth's surface, beavers began to diminish in size. Scientists speculate that as food became scarce in the colder climate, the largest beaver cubs in each successive litter could not find enough food to survive and reproduce. The runts of the litter did survive, however, and passed on the genetic code for small size. As the cold continued for thousands of generations, the size of the average beaver decreased, until it reached a level where survival was no longer problematic. The modern-day beaver is relatively diminutive, tipping the scales at twenty-six to ninety pounds and reaching a standing height of thirty-four to fifty-four inches—about the size of a large dog.

Beavers are best known for their ability to create ponds, which are their major defense against predators. To make one, beavers must first build a dam across a stream or rivulet. This floods the area upstream of the dam. Choosing a suitable site for the dam is critical. Beavers sometimes pick the wrong location, and the water washes around the dam or flows off in a new direction instead of forming a shallow pond. Other times, the pond may block a road, causing problems for the beaver's human neighbors.

After the dam site is chosen, the job of felling trees begins. The beaver selects a tree, then perches on its hind feet and, grasping the trunk with its front paws, bites into the tree with two long, orange, chisel-shaped upper teeth. The beaver then uses its lower front teeth to gnaw away the wood. The two upper teeth remain jammed into the wood until it has been removed by the lower teeth. The next bite puts the upper teeth deeper into the wood. The beaver thus digs a V-shaped notch deeper and deeper into the tree, until it completely encircles the tree and the tree begins to sway. Although beavers

Tail braced against the ground, a beaver has no problem quickly cutting down even a young tree.

are masters at cutting trees, they cannot judge the direction the tree will take as it falls. Amazingly, most beavers can waddle away fast enough to get out of the way, but there are sometimes accidents.

Aside from their use as building material, another reason for cutting down trees is for food. The tender, growing wood tissue just beneath the bark is an important food supply for the beaver. Beavers are primarily bark eaters, eating the bark from tender twigs and the new growth (cambium layer) that lies between the old outer bark and the wood. In the summer, beavers forage for plants along the pond's muddy bottom, where they are safe from land-based predators. Nonwoody foods there include roots and rhizomes of aquatic plants, such as lily, watercress, bur reed, and arrowhead. Beavers' front paws are excellent tools for digging up these delicacies. A beaver eats about one and one-half to two pounds of food a day.

The trees cut down are usually about three to five inches in diameter, and the beaver can fell them in a matter of minutes. A record for beavers was established in British Columbia, where they cut down a 110-foot-tall cotton-wood with a diameter of about seven inches.

Once they've constructed a dam, the next project for the beavers is to build a lodge. The beavers usually build their lodge in the pond that develops

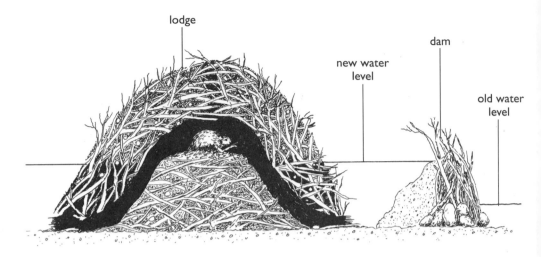

Cross section of a beaver dam and lodge

lodge

new water
level

dam

old water
level

on the downstream side of the dam. The pond surrounding the lodge acts as a moat that effectively keeps away most predators most of the time, although an occasional mink has been known to cross the pond and slip undetected into the lodge to capture a young beaver for dinner. They may also build their lodge in a mudbank or in an existing shallow pond, lake, or marsh, but wherever the lodge is built, the water must be four feet or more deep so the beavers can come and go without exposing themselves to danger.

The pond also helps beavers survive the winter. Even though beavers store a supply of tender branches and saplings in the lodge, they may need to gather more food before the end of the cold season. If the pond is partially frozen, they can swim under the ice, where they can breathe oxygen from air trapped in a layer between the ice and the water. If water freezes to the bottom of the pond, however, the beavers would be trapped in the lodge. Beavers can protect themselves from this when they construct the dam. The higher the dam, the deeper the pond, and the less likely the water will be to freeze throughout its depth.

The lodge is constructed from small logs, branches, and twigs, with mud holding it all together. Sometimes the beavers also include wet vegetation. Lodges vary in size, but they generally don't exceed seven feet in height and forty feet in diameter.

A beaver colony is a family group consisting of a pair of beavers mated for life, plus yearlings and newborn kits. Thus the beaver work crew during the construction of a new dam and lodge can be a considerable size. The usual size of the litters is two to four, although they may range in size from one to nine. Males may leave the lodge following the birth of a new litter, but they return later in the year. Kits mature in one and one-half to two years, at which time they are encouraged to leave the lodge.

Beavers' expertise at building extends far beyond the construction of a dam and a lodge. When the supply of timber for the dam along the banks of the stream is exhausted, they need to find suitable supplies elsewhere. This often requires the beavers to dig canals deep into the woods. In these water-filled trenches, beavers float the timber downstream to the construction site. During this period, beavers can be exposed to dangers, so to avoid becoming the next meal of a hungry predator, they dig a temporary living space in the mud along the banks. In certain areas within their range, beavers may live permanently in such bankside lodges.

Beavers are marvels of physical design. They can travel through the water at a top speed of six miles per hour, although their cruising speed is considerably slower, about two miles per hour. The back feet each have flexible webbing between the five toes, similar to that on a duck's foot. The webbing gives the beaver the same advantage that swim fins give the human swimmer. When swimming, the beaver alternately extends its hind legs down and away from the body. As each foot pushes against the water, the toes spread apart, exposing the webbing. Sometimes the beaver extends both back feet at the same time, which propels the animal more leisurely through the water.

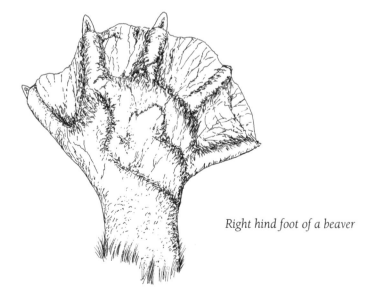

Right hind foot of a beaver

A beaver can remain underwater for fifteen minutes and can cover half a mile before it needs to refill its lungs with air. It can accomplish these extraordinary physical feats because of dramatic physiological capabilities. As soon as the animal dives, its heart rate is reduced by half. In addition, its body can tolerate carbon dioxide buildup that would be lethal to us. When the beaver surfaces, it takes only a couple of deep breaths to clear the lungs of carbon dioxide and fill them with fresh air.

The two delicate front paws don't play a major role in swimming. The beaver folds them into fists, which it keeps close to its head. In this position, the fists act as bumpers to push away debris floating in the water. The front paws each have five toes with long, strong claws, like the hind feet, but they have no webbing. Beavers can manipulate these front paws so well that it is almost tempting to think of them as hands. They are excellent for digging, grooming, and handling construction material when the beaver is building. They also serve the beaver well as it rolls twigs while gnawing, similar to the way we roll a cob of corn when eating it.

It was once thought that the beaver's large, nine- to seventeen-inch-long, paddle-shaped tail was used as a small shovel to plaster mud onto dams and lodges when building or repairing, but observations of beavers in the wild showed this to be untrue. The tail, covered with leathery scales and dotted with a few coarse hairs, is used as a rudder when swimming to help steer the animal through the water. The beaver also uses its tail as a stool to sit on when gnawing a piece of alder or surveying the countryside.

Other adaptations also add to the beaver's success in the water. The nose and small ears are equipped with valves that close when the animal is submerged. Each of the small, brown eyes has a transparent lid that closes when underwater, similar to our use of a mask or goggles. On land, the beaver loses some visual acuity.

Although beavers do not have long, sharp claws or sharp teeth set in powerful jaws, they are not helpless. When endangered, a beaver slaps its tail on the water, creating an explosive crack. This warning signal carries for long distances and is passed rapidly from one beaver group to another. The series of slaps grows progressively fainter as the distance from its origin increases.

The heavy cascade of water that follows a vigorous slap also has immediate consequences for a predator that has ventured a little too close, and the few seconds it takes for the startled hungry beast to recover allows the beaver time to dive out of harm's way. The more vigorous the beaver, the more resounding the slap and the greater the splash. Together, these signal the predator that this is a feisty fellow and perhaps it should look elsewhere for a meal.

Although they travel on four legs, beavers cannot run swiftly under the best of conditions. Sometimes they are forced to live in a pond surrounded by a thickly wooded area with a tangle of underbrush. Knowing that they can't get around well in these conditions, the beavers build a plunge hole leading to their water-based lodge. These tunnels can be as far as fifty feet from the water's edge. Except during extreme drought, the tunnels are always flooded, a fact that stops most predators.

Beavers also have a silent signal system to warn off would-be intruders, often young homesteading beavers that have left their parents' lodge. When entering territory occupied by a colony of beavers, these travelers encounter scent mounds, piles of mud at the water's edge. Members of the colony each deposit their scent on the mound, thereby claiming the territory and declaring the area off-limits to transients. Scent marking is a peaceful way to claim a section of the watershed, preventing fights over boundaries. This is important, since a fighting beaver can inflict a lethal blow with its incisors.

Although beavers have a reputation for being hard, diligent workers, careful observations over extended periods of time have shown a more relaxed lifestyle. Beavers work on construction jobs or at gathering food to fill the larders for only about five hours of the day. Throughout this relatively short workday, the beavers take breaks from work periodically to snack or to snooze.

Beavers change the face of the land. A stream once flanked by mature trees and a tangle of undergrowth disappears, and a pond appears where there was none. As the roots of the remaining trees become flooded, they die. In a few years, cattails, water lilies, and other moisture-loving plants move into the place that was once home to trees and shrubs. The shallow water attracts waterfowl, while the snags of dead trees become home to raccoons, owls, and other wild creatures. Turtles and snakes also move in to this nurturing habitat.

After many generations of beavers living in a lodge, food becomes scarce in the area, and the beavers leave. The pond dries. In the rich mud, a variety of new plants take hold. In time, the pond fills with soil. A meadow supporting a rich community of wildflowers eventually appears. Many meadows that flourish close to wetlands began in this way.

Muskrats (*Ondatra zibethica*) also frequent wet places. They are active at night, though they may be out in the day during the late spring and early summer. You are likely to see them when it rains. Unlike beavers, which prefer open streams, muskrats favor swampy areas with still or slow-running water, with vegetation growing in the water or along the shore. Muskrats also live in saltwater marshes along the East Coast and in coastal Louisiana and Mississippi. The name muskrat comes from their scaly, hairless, ratlike tails

Muskrats look like overgrown field mice that have adapted to life in the water.

and the musky odor they spray from scent glands during mating season. Both male and female muskrats apply this "perfume" around their breeding sites.

Muskrats are smaller than beavers, measuring sixteen to twenty-five inches from nose to tail. They rarely weigh more than three pounds, and they look like huge mice. They have thick, glossy fur that's dark blackish brown over their backs. The sides are lighter brown and sometimes have a reddish or yellowish tinge. The adults molt continuously, but the young molt only once during their first year.

Muskrats are well adapted to an aquatic lifestyle. They can swim underwater for twelve to seventeen minutes before they have to return to the surface for a gasp of air, although the usual time spent underwater is two to three minutes. The muskrat has partially webbed hind feet that help in swimming. The muskrat tail also aids in swimming. With flattened sides, it makes a fine rudder used for steering the muskrat through the water. A fold of skin protects the inner ears from water, adding to the animal's adaptability in the water.

Some muskrats live a solitary life, but others live with their mates during most of the year. Muskrats are fickle, however, and may mate frequently. One female may produce three litters a year. If a male stays with a female, he may use his sharp teeth to inflict fatal wounds on an intruder. Muskrats are not social animals, but they will warn each other by slapping their tails on the water if danger approaches. Unlike the affable beavers, muskrats can be fighters that will defend their territories even if their life is the price. They are quarrelsome and always ready for a squabble. Food seems to be the trigger for their pugnacious behavior. When plenty of food is available, there is little bickering. The adults are vocal and give loud squeals, snarls, and squeaks. Young muskrats have squeaky cries.

Muskrats live in burrows that they dig in banks along the margins of ponds, streams, and swamps. These bank burrows are about six inches high and eight inches wide. A tunnel, ten to fifty feet long, extends from a dry chamber and usually opens underwater. When dry periods decrease the level of the surrounding water, muskrats build a canal connecting the tunnel with deeper water. The water needs to be deep enough that it won't freeze to the bottom, but not so deep that submerged vegetation does not grow in it.

When living in a marsh or pond, muskrats build mound-shaped lodges on platforms of mud piled with cattails, sedges, small sticks, leaves, and any other type of vegetation found in the area. The lodge begins as a heap of vegetation. When the heap is about two feet high, the muskrats begin to dig out the interior. Sometimes these lodges are washed away by floods, but new ones are built in late summer or early fall.

During dry periods, when the water level lowers, muskrat burrows may be more easily seen along the banks of streams and margins of ponds or swamps.

*Cross section of
a muskrat lodge*

Muskrats also create feeding stations made of heaps of sticks. These are frequently mistaken for lodges, which they resemble. Discarded clam or mussel shells and cut vegetation in the area may indicate this muskrat behavior. In winter, muskrats often create "push-ups," mounds of vegetation that cover holes in the ice and protect the animal from the cold as it eats food found underwater. In summer, when a pond may dry up, muskrats can live without drinking water by eating succulents when they are available. Young muskrats do not fare as well. Many of them die of thirst because the water available in the succulents is not adequate for their needs.

Muskrats dine largely on stems, leaves, and rootstocks of marsh plants, such as broad-leaved arrowhead, cattails, bur reed, panic grass, cut-grass, rice, and water lilies. Duckweed, when available, provides about 90 percent of their nutritional needs, as well as effective camouflage. When available, they will also eat blueberries, wild rice, white clover, corn, bluegrass, wild celery, muskgrass, cheatgrass, and even cultivated garden plants. Although primarily vegetarians, muskrats will also eat mussels, clams, snails, crayfish, fish, frogs, reptiles, and young birds. Even dead muskrats are acceptable fare.

Muskrats do not hibernate in winter, but they stay close to home. They patrol beneath the ice for plant and animal food, but if the water freezes below the underwater openings to the lodge, the muskrats are in grave trouble, because they may not be able to gnaw through the ice to get food. If their reserve food is depleted, in desperation they will eat the sticks and twigs

THE PLAYERS

that make up their lodge. In time, they will eat through the walls of the lodge, then have to begin looking for another shelter, perhaps a vacant beaver lodge or feeding station. Some muskrats survive these difficult times; others become food for hungry predators such as otters, weasels, minks, marsh hawks, great horned owls, and fish such as northern pike.

Raccoons (*Procyon lotor*) are smart nocturnal mammals that live in marshy places and wooded areas bordering the banks of streams and rivers. Humans have destroyed much of these natural habitats, but unlike beavers and muskrats, raccoons have found other suitable places to live. As long as there is adequate food and water, farmlands, urban parks, and suburban backyards have become home to these adaptable animals, which may inhabit church steeples, sewers, sheds, and even parking garages. In the wild, raccoons spend the winter in dens, which are usually located in tree hollows. They also may overwinter in caves, rock crevices, rotting logs, cavities beneath tree roots, or beneath clumps of dried marsh grass.

From nose to tail, raccoons measure twenty-six to thirty-eight inches. Males weigh eight to twenty-five pounds, and females weigh six and three-quarters to seventeen and one-half pounds. Their coat is made up of two different kinds of hair—short, fine hair, which forms a dense undercover (90 percent), and longer, coarser guard hair, which gives the raccoon its color (10 percent). Raccoon fur is composed of a variety of colors, including shades of black, brown, gray, and even a touch of yellow. The raccoon is easy to identify, with its distinctive black mask and ringed tail.

Female raccoon with kits

Male raccoons generally mate with more than one female during the breeding season. Between sixty and seventy-three days after mating, the female raccoon gives birth to three to seven kits. Most are born in April. The tiny, hairless young enter the world with their eyes and ears sealed and must wait about eighteen days before they can see their mother, who is an attentive caregiver. Kits usually stay with their mother through the summer and fall and sleep with her through the winter. In the spring, the mother chases the kits away as the competition for food and space grows keen.

Raccoons eat a variety of plant and animal foods. Typically, about 75 percent of the raccoon diet consists of plant material, and only 25 percent is food from animals. In the spring, summer, and fall, raccoons forage for grasses, raspberries, blackberries, pokeberries, blueberries, acorns, corn, nuts, insects,

Raccoons feast on sweet wild grapes.

earthworms, and crayfish. They will also dine on deer mice, baby rabbits, meadow voles, turtles, and ground-nesting birds and their eggs. These opportunistic mammals also eat almost anything they can find in garbage cans and are becoming especially fond of the remains of ice cream, cakes, pies, and other junk food. Predators include red foxes, coyotes, wolves, bobcats, fishers, and great horned owls.

Raccoons are vocal creatures, as their human neighbors can verify. Anyone who lives within the range of some raccoons has likely heard the variety of sounds that these animals can make. When loud snarls and growls tear through the silence of the night, we usually think the neighborhood dogs are doing battle with one another, but if you follow the noise to the source, you may discover that the noise is coming from quarreling raccoons. When angry or frightened, a raccoon can also hiss like a goose. If you witness one of these squabbles, describe the sounds. How do they change during the battle?

THE WORLD OF WETLAND MAMMALS

What you will need	Science skills
basic kit	observing
binoculars	recording
camera	inferring

OBSERVATIONS

Beavers were reorganizing and redesigning the landscape long before human beings got into the business. The activities presented here encourage you to look at how beavers do their work and get a peek at the family life of these affectionate rodents. Raccoons and muskrats share the beavers' habitat. As you look for beavers, you may have an opportunity to observe these other mammals.

Dam Construction. When beavers move into a new area that lacks a pond, they construct a dam across a stream or river to restrict the flow of water and create a pond upstream of the dam. After beavers have selected a site for the dam, they begin felling trees. When a tree is down, the beaver trims off large branches, drags the log to the stream, and guides it to the dam site.

Beavers lay the first logs side by side and jam them into the mud, with the butt ends facing downstream. In this position, the remaining branches catch debris and mud floating downstream, adding to the width of the dam. On this foundation, beavers pile anything they can find, such as sticks, stones, and wood chips, onto the upstream side of the dam. The downstream side of the dam is made primarily of sticks and branches. The beavers then fill the spaces between the upstream materials with mud and vegetation.

Explore ponds near your home, looking for beaver dams. If you find such a dam, look at the materials the beavers used. Write the materials you observe in your notebook. Do you see evidence of human discards, such as automobile or bicycle tires, lumber, plastic, bottles, or cans? How long is the dam? How high above the water level of the pond is it? How high is it above the downstream side? How wide is the crest? Does the dam cross the stream in a straight line or does it zigzag? Can you find any evidence that the crest of the dam has been used as a bridge by animals such as muskrats or raccoons?

Examining a dam that is broken will give you a better appreciation for the skills required for building. If you come across such a dam, take some time to study its design. Make a drawing or photograph it for your field notebook. Can you identify some of the building materials the beavers used?

Lodge Construction. Dome-shaped lodges are crafted from piles of sticks that are plastered with mud and debris. The summer heat bakes the muddy mortar, which is further hardened by the winter freeze. The lodge offers excellent protection for the beavers that live there. Fresh air enters the structure through cracks left in the roof, which are loosely covered with vegetation. The air is circulated by the surging and heaving of water at the underwater entrance holes to the lodge.

Beavers dig mud and debris with their front paws, roll it into balls, and carry them to the construction site, where they smear the mud into place. The lodge may eventually extend more than six feet above the surface of the pond, and the diameter may exceed thirty-six feet. More than one generation will live in a lodge, and each succeeding generation adds to its size. What is the height of the lodges you find? The diameter?

Not all beavers live in pond-based lodges; some excavate bank burrows, often complexes of tunnels in the banks of slow-moving streams. The underwater openings are about a foot in diameter. As you wander in beaver country, look for these bankside dens.

Canals. Beavers often build canals to help them move logs to a construction site. The canals also offer the beaver protection from land-based predators. The canals may be two feet wide and two feet deep. Do you see any canals leading to the beaver pond?

Beaver Families. Beavers live in a family unit called a colony, made up of a breeding pair that mate for life, yearlings, and newborn kits. While they live

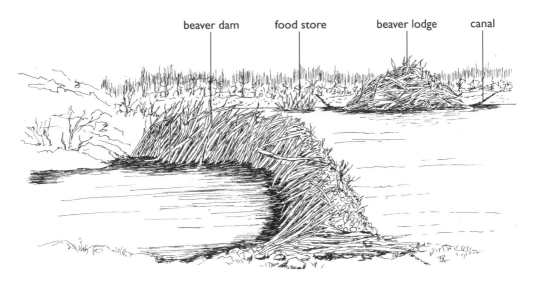

beaver dam   food store   beaver lodge   canal

The beaver dam provides a pond in which to construct the lodge. Underwater tunnels lead to the living chamber. Branches stored nearby provide winter food. Canals help the beaver move logs to the building site.

with their parents, young beavers practice valuable skills and learn inter-family cooperation, a behavior essential to their lifestyle. At two years of age, the young beavers leave the lodge and set out to find mates and establish family units of their own.

It is said that beavers are affectionate with each other. What do you see that supports this statement? Do you observe beavers engaged in play? Do you see them rubbing noses with one another? Do you observe other signs of affection between them?

Finding Evidence of Beavers. Beaver tracks are difficult to find, because they are usually smeared by the beaver's tail as it walks in mud. Unlike most other rodents, beavers have five toes on their front and back feet, but because of their tendency to drag objects to and from their lodge, you will generally see only four toes on their footprints, as the fifth toe on each foot is usually obliterated by drag marks. However, the identifiable impression made by their claws is a strong clue that beavers were there. Another clue are the two knobs in the heel portion of the print. You may also find drag marks in the mud made by the heavy tail.

Another sign indicating the presence of beavers is gnawed tree stumps. You may see stumps that are higher than a beaver could normally stand while

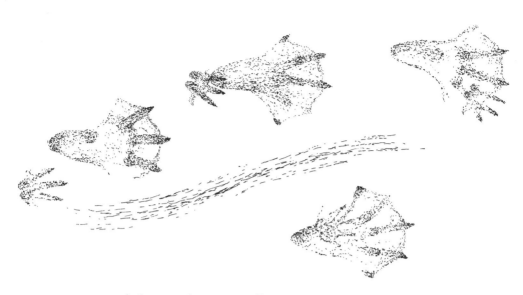

The beaver's alternating walking patterns can be irregular.

gnawing at the tree. This happens when the beaver is felling a tree while standing on several feet of snow.

Another clue to the presence of beavers is the marks made by the two large front teeth, or incisors, in the upper and lower jaws. You can suspect their presence if you see tooth marks in the bark of aspen, poplar, willow, birch, maple, cottonwood, willow, hickory, oaks (white, red, and black), black gum, flowering dogwood, serviceberry, willow shrubs, or wild grapevines. The beaver's incisors each measure one-quarter to one-half inch wide. This measurement will help you determine whether gnawing marks you observe on a tree were made by a beaver or some other gnawing animal.

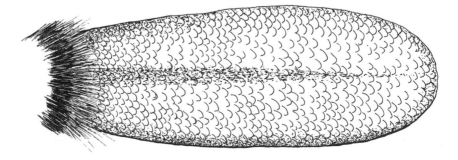

When swimming, the beaver's broad, scale-covered tail is used as a rudder.

The beaver's incisor teeth are for gnawing and are characteristic of all rodents.

Gnawed tree stumps generally mean that beavers are in the area.

BEAVERS, MUSKRATS, AND RACCOONS

Paths and mudslides may be another clue to the presence of beavers. Beavers make paths, usually ten to twelve inches wide, from their pond to feeding grounds or another wetland. You can usually identify a path by the trimmed shrubs along its edge, wood chips along the path, and drag marks made by the beaver's tail. Through heavy use, the paths become worn and end in mudslides at the pond's edge. Look for them as you survey a beaver pond. How many mudslides can you find?

In the winter, although beavers do not hibernate, in the northern part of their range they may leave the lodge only to get some food that they anchored underwater in the mud before the pond froze. The islands of branches jutting above the ice in front of the lodge are evidence of their activity and tell you the beavers are probably home. Look for them.

Adult beavers often make soft churrs, hisses, whines, mumbles, and nasal noises. The young may be heard making high-pitched whines. Listen for these sounds when you are in beaver country.

Observing Beavers. Beavers have blunt heads and small eyes and ears. With a stout body and short legs, it's impossible for the beaver to run quickly. Some say that beavers waddle. Do you agree? A pair of binoculars will help you get a better look at them. They are graceful and swift underwater, but this is not so easy to observe.

Beaver fur is chestnut to dark brown, but in the northern part of their range, it's almost black. The coat is designed to keep the beaver dry and warm, even though the beaver spends a great deal of time in the water. Beneath the long, coarse guard hairs lies an undercoat of shorter, finer fur of a lighter color than the guard hairs. This underfur is thickest on the beaver's back and gives the coat its softness and resistance to wetness. Beavers are never wet to their skin, no matter how much they dive or how long they swim.

If you have a dog that has these two types of hair, you can easily examine the differences between the guard hairs and the soft fur of the undercoat. To see how well the undercoat works at keeping the animal dry, give the dog a bath. The addition of soap to the bath water helps get the undercoat wet.

Grooming. The two inside toes of each foot of the beaver are equipped with specialized claws that serve as combs. Beavers comb their fur, dislodge parasites, and waterproof their fur with oil from their anal glands. In the wild, you won't be able to see these "combs," but you may be able to observe the grooming act. If you do, take a series of photographs to show the process. Is there an order to it? What part of the body does the beaver groom first? What part is groomed last?

Eyes. If you shine a flashlight at the eyes of a dog, they glow like burning

The two inside toenails on each back foot are split and are good for combing the beaver's coat.

double claws

coals. This does not occur with beavers. The eyes of dogs, like raccoons, have a reflective membrane called the tapetum lucidum, which lets them make the most use of available light. The trade-off for this ability to see in dim light is that images are less clear. Often you see the eyes of these animals glowing red in the beam of car headlights or a flashlight. This is called eye shine and is the result of the light reflecting off the tapetum lucidum.

If you shine a flashlight beam at beavers' eyes, they do not glow, as they lack the light-gathering membrane of many other nocturnal creatures. They see in the dark much as we do—not terribly well.

There is some speculation about the reason for this. Records of early observations indicate that the beaver was once quite active during some part of the day, and it was referred to as a diurnal animal. Some scientists think their nocturnal behavior is a fairly recent response to the species' survival being threatened by trappers.

Muskrat Footprints. Look for footprints in the soft mud that surrounds the muskrat habitat. Compare muskrat footprints with those of a cat or dog. What differences do you notice? Make a drawing of the prints in your field notebook. Explain how its webbed feet help the muskrat in the water. Do you see any evidence of muskrat predators, such as otters or minks?

Coat. Describe the fur. Compare it with the fur of a raccoon or a water-loving dog like a Labrador retriever. Is the muskrat better fitted for life in the water or on land? A pair of binoculars may help you get a close look at the muskrat's fur.

Feet. Where did you discover the tracks of the muskrat? Write a description of the area. Measure the width and length of the print of one foot. What is the width between the prints of the two hind feet? What is the length between the prints made by the hind feet in several successive steps? How do these measurements compare to those of a raccoon, cat, or dog? Can you tell

Right hind foot of a muskrat showing partial webbing

Muskrat walking pattern is similar to that of a woodchuck. The hind track registers close to or partially on top of the front track.

if the muskrat was walking, running, or jumping? Do the feet tell you if the muskrat is a good swimmer?

Raccoon Footprints. Raccoons forage along streams and muddy riverbanks during summer and fall. If the watercourse is affected by tides, the best time to look for footprints is at low tide. Raccoon tracks are easy to identify, because the animals walk on the soles of their feet with the heels touching the ground, much like bears and humans. Raccoon prints look a lot like those of

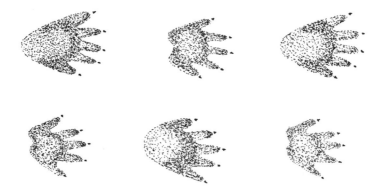

The lumbering walk of a raccoon is unique. The front and hind feet alternate sides in each group of tracks. Look for the two-by-two pattern.

a small child. When you find some footprints, try to tell a story about the foraging animals. How many were there? Did any of them come nose to nose with each other?

Finding Raccoons. When looking for tree dens, remember that tree holes don't have to be large; even large raccoons can fit through amazingly small holes. Look for scat on the ground around the tree and for grizzled brown fur on the tree bark. If there is a cover of snow on the ground, raccoon footprints are another clue.

A raccoon may choose a different spot each day for sunning itself or sleeping. Daytime resting sites may be in buildings, wooded areas, or wetlands such as swamps or salt marshes. Because they enjoy sunning themselves, look for them along the banks of streams and ponds. Tree limbs or even abandoned squirrel nests are also highly desirable resting places. If you find a raccoon curled up on the branch of a tree, you will discover what good camouflage

Raccoons generally select tree hollows as den sites.

*Raccoons are good
tree climbers.*

the ringed tail offers the animal as it naps. Raccoons are known to leave a resting place to forage shortly after sunset and return to it or a different place an hour or so before sunrise. Look for resting places in your area. How long after sunset does the raccoon leave the resting place?

Tree Climbing. Raccoons climb tree trunks to reach their dens, find a resting spot, or escape danger. If it's not in a hurry, how does the raccoon use its feet? If the raccoon is being chased, it will leap up the tree. Describe the way it moves its feet. (See Chapter Note 1.)

Raccoons can descend a tree headfirst. Like other animals that climb down trees, raccoons turn their hind feet outward so that their claws can grasp the trunk more easily. For comparison, observe a squirrel as it races down a tree trunk.

Raccoons also can back down a tree. When they do this, you will see them use their feet alternately as they do when making a leisurely ascent.

Close-up of a Raccoon. When you find a raccoon, take some time to observe it. A pair of binoculars is helpful, especially if the raccoon is some distance away from you. Does the raccoon have a stocky build, or is its body streamlined like a squirrel? Is its nose pointed? Describe its ears. Can the raccoon turn them in the direction of a sound? What color are its eyes? How many rings are on its tail? How long is it? Is the tail longer or shorter than the raccoon's body? (See Chapter Note 2.)

Raccoon Body Language. Raccoons can express themselves through body language. Look for the following expressions as you observe raccoons at work and at play:

general annoyance: tail lashing and whipping violently

threat: baring teeth and laying back ears, raising shoulder hackles, arching back, and raising tail

submission: lowering entire body to ground and backing away from aggressor

general annoyance

threat

submission

CHAPTER NOTES

1. Climbing. When leisurely climbing a tree, a raccoon will use its feet alternately; it places its right hind foot beside its left forefoot. Despite their size, raccoons make their way through the trees with the agility of squirrels. If a raccoon loses its balance it will grab onto a branch and dangle momentarily, then secure the branch with the claws of its four feet and proceed along in a slothlike fashion.

2. Close-up of a Raccoon. The total length of a raccoon from the tip of its nose to the tip of its tail can be from twenty-six to thirty-eight inches. Its ringed tail is generally between twelve inches long and may have five to seven dark rings. This tail is used primarily for balance when the raccoon is climbing trees or walking along the branches but also serves as a muffler when sleeping in cold weather and affords camouflage to a raccoon resting in sun-dappled foliage.

Male raccoons weigh between eight and twenty-five pounds, and females weigh between six and three-quarters and seventeen and one-half pounds. Raccoons weigh less in the spring and more in the fall. Raccoons that live in the Florida Keys are smaller, usually weighing a mere three to six pounds and rarely exceeding eight pounds. Raccoons in Wisconsin have been reported to weigh as much as sixty-two pounds, but some experts don't believe this figure.

Selected Bibliography

THE STAGE

Platt, Rutherford. *Water: The Wonder of Life.* Englewood Cliffs, N. J.: Prentice-Hall Inc., 1971.

National Geographic Special Edition. Water: The Power, Promise and Turmoil of North America's Fresh Water. November, 1993.

THE PLAYERS

Borror, Donald J., and Richard E. White. *A Field Guide to the Insects.* Boston: Houghton Mifflin, 1970.

Brockman, Frank. *Trees of North America.* New York: Golden Press, 1976.

Burt, William H., and Richard P. Grossenheider. *A Field Guide to the Mammals.* Boston: Houghton Mifflin, 1976.

Caduto, Michael. *Pond and Brook: A Guide to Nature in Freshwater Environments.* Hanover: University Press of New England, 1985.

Cobb, Boughton. *Peterson Field Guide: Ferns.* New York: Houghton Mifflin, 1984.

Conant, Roger, and Joseph Collins. *Peterson Field Guide to Reptiles and Amphibians of Eastern/Central North America.* New York: Houghton Mifflin, 1998.

Cvancara, Alan M. *At the Water's Edge.* New York: John Wiley & Sons, Inc., 1989.

Glassberg, Jeffrey. *Butterflies Through Binoculars.* New York: Oxford University Press, 1993.

Green, N. Bayard, and Thomas K. Pauley. *Amphibians and Reptiles in West Virginia.* Pittsburgh, PA: University of Pittsburgh Press, 1987.

Klemens, Michael W. *Amphibians and Reptiles of Connecticut and Adjacent Regions.* State Geological and Natural History Survey of Connecticut, 1993.

Malcolm, L. Hunter, Jr., John Albright, and Jane Arbuckle, eds. *The Amphibians and Reptiles of Maine.* Orno, ME: Maine Agricultural Experiment Station, University of Maine, 1992.

Martof, Bernard S., William M. Palmer, Joseph R. Bailey, and Julian R. Harrison III. *Amphibians and Reptiles of the Carolinas and Virginia.* Chapel Hill, NC: The University of North Carolina Press, 1980.

Newcomb, Lawrence. *Wildflower Guide.* Boston: Little, Brown and Company, 1977.

Petranka, James W. *Salamanders of the United States and Canada.* Washington, DC: Smithsonian Institution Press, 1998.

Pfingsten, Ralph A., and Floyd L. Downs, eds. *Salamanders of Ohio.* Columbus, OH: College of Biological Sciences, Ohio State University, 1989.

Opler, Paul A., and Vichai Malikul. *Peterson Field Guide: Eastern Butterflies.* New York: Houghton Mifflin, 1992.

Ryden, Hope. *Lily Pond: Four Years with a Family of Beavers.* Rockville, MD: Lyons Press, 1997.

Wright, Amy Bartlett. *Peterson First Field Guides: Caterpillars.* Boston: Houghton Mifflin, 1993.

Xerces Society and Smithsonian Institution. *Butterfly Gardening.* San Francisco: Sierra Club Books, 1990.